Why Community Matters

Why Community Matters
Connecting Education with Civic Life

Nicholas V. Longo

State University of New York Press

Published by
State University of New York Press, Albany

For information, contact State University of New York Press, Albany, NY
www.sunypress.edu

Production by Kelli Williams
Marketing by Fran Keneston

Library of Congress Cataloguing-in-Publication Data

Longo, Nicholas V., 1974–
    Why community matters : connecting education with civic life /
Nicholas V. Longo.
        p. cm.
    Includes bibliographical references and index.
    ISBN 978-0-7914-7197-5 (hardcover : alk. paper) — ISBN 978-0-7914-7198-2
(pbk. : alk. paper)   1. Community and school—United States.   2. Education—
Aims and objectives—United States.   I. Title.

LC221.L66   2007
370.11'5—dc22

2006101102

10 9 8 7 6 5 4 3

For Mom and Dad, Paula and Nick Sr.,
and
for Aleida and Maya

Contents

Preface

The idea for this book began, without my knowing it, when as an undergraduate student I was invited to participate outside what sometimes felt like the "bubble" of the college campus in several courses that included community service. I soon became immersed in community problem-solving as an undergraduate and then as a graduate student working at the Center for Democracy and Citizenship at the University of Minnesota. These experiences introduced me to a new educational method as well as a different kind of politics.

The relationships I formed across age, race, class, and cultural differences with people outside the campus were different from those I had with a teacher and my peers in the classroom. Both were learning relationships, but my experiences in the community allowed me to see more diverse perspectives; they also had more public and productive dimensions.

Learning in a community context was actually very natural and powerful, especially as I began to ask people to tell stories of meaningful learning experiences, along with stories of how they formed civic identities. Most, like me, engaged in meaningful learning outside the confines of the school building. People also tend to learn about public issues in community settings, like the local pizzerias, delis, and barber shops where I discussed the issues of the day growing up in Yonkers, New York.

Simply put, I learned that it takes a village to educate a citizen. This idea is founded on the premise that schools are essential for the civic growth of children, but inadequate to the educational equation. Communities must also be educative. I've since realized that, as a society, we're not doing so well at this. We rely too much on a single institution to solve all of our problems. Education has become confused with schooling. This is also true for the most fundamental of challenges: educating for democracy.

While "civic education" is now a buzzword among policy makers and educators concerned about the state of our democracy, especially the disconnection of young people from public life, this field of endeavor is often too narrowly defined. Aside from the focus on schooling and curriculum, civic education tends to promote the easiest things to count—voting, volunteer hours, and the acquisition of civic knowledge. When this happens, civic learning is an isolated project, not part of a broader culture of democratic engagement. And, perhaps most significant, civic education becomes about getting young people to participate in the system as it is, rather than helping to create a different kind of public life.

Yet there is a great possibility for a more expansive approach to civic learning. My experience with a different type of education and politics, of course, is by no means unique. There is an emerging movement for a citizen-centered democracy in an array of fields, including education, as Harry Boyte, Peter Levine, Carmen Sirianni, Cynthia Gibson and others have documented.[1] What might be less apparent, however, is that this movement is part of a long tradition of citizens using education to build democratic communities.

This book is an attempt to introduce a conception of learning and civic life in which education for democracy is a function of whole communities. To accomplish this, I draw on both the current and historical examples that see the importance of community in educating for democracy and argue for an ecological approach to civic learning. This conception traces back to the late nineteenth century with the settlement house movement and Jane Addams's Hull House in urban Chicago, and then directly ties to the civil rights movement of the 1950s and 1960s with the educational efforts of the Highlander Folk School in rural Tennessee. These traditions, fortunately, are still very much alive in communities around the country, most especially on the West Side of St. Paul in a community-based civic learning experiment called the Neighborhood Learning Community.

Education as the function of whole communities is about more than standardized tests, and it involves more than preparation for the workplace. It is also about more than preparing people to be part of the system "as it is." This book attempts to tell stories that run counter the dominant political, educational, and research narratives.

First and foremost, this book invites the possibility of a different kind of politics in striking contrast with the zero-sum "politics as usual" that today has created a divisive, bitter landscape of Red and Blue America. Moving beyond a limited scarcity model toward a politics of abundance means a transformation of our public life. Public life, then, is about creative possibility and the many resources in a community.

But getting to this different kind of politics requires a change in the way we view civic education. It seems that education is the ideal arena to transform civic life. Education for democracy cannot be a passive experience; it must be engaged. And education, more than any other endeavor, allows us to see the whole as more than individual parts. Quite simply, there is much to gain by reaching beyond the schools to make education the function of the entire community.

Thus, this book makes an important claim about education policy. I examine the connection between education, community, and democracy—and provide an important alternative to the emphasis on high-stakes testing and school-based accountability measures that dominate the current national educational policy debates.

Finally, seeing the value in this different approach to politics and education requires seeing the importance of a new kind of epistemology. Learning and knowledge creation outside of the traditional classroom, of course, are a challenge to the very way we know. Like the civic actors I write about in this book, I do not attempt to present "objective" data or "quantifiable" findings; rather, this research embodies my belief that as a practitioner and scholar, my work is based on living relationships with people—I see the sometimes subtle power of people telling their own stories.

Relationships are at the core of educating for democracy, and relationships can be at the core of engaged research. Research need not be detached; it can be engaged and concerned. As engaged scholarship, my aim is to continue a conversation, rather than discover a truth. I have tried, to use Herman Blake's wonderful phrase, to "listen eloquently" and then describe accurately and compellingly the stories that follow.[2]

Acknowledgments

My experience in researching and writing this book has only confirmed for me that community matters, as I have been supported by a group of colleagues, friends, and family to whom I am deeply grateful. This book, in many ways, is a continuation of our ongoing conversations.

First, I want to thank the Center for Information and Research on Civic Learning and Engagement (CIRCLE) for recognizing the importance of the community dimension of civic learning and funding this project at an early stage. I especially want to thank Peter Levine for his encouragement and ongoing support, along with Abby Kiesa, William Galston, and Mark Lopez.

I was also generously supported by the Charles F. Kettering Foundation that helped this material take shape as a book, and I am especially grateful to David Mathews and John Dedrick. Kettering's vast civic network also had a great impact on my thinking about democracy, including Guillermo Correa, Carolyn Farrow-Garland, Laura Hall, Valarie Lemmie, Ileana Marin, Randy Nielsen, Hal Saunders, and Maxine Thomas.

My work with the Center for Democracy and Citizenship grounds my understanding of the central role that citizens can play in public life. Harry Boyte is a great mentor who guided me through the various stages of this book; his belief in the possibility of ordinary citizens, along with his ability to build a practical philosophy of democratic politics, continue to inspire. So, too, does Nan Skelton, a savvy and energetic organizer, who always sees possibilities for community.

Jerry Stein pushed me to strengthen my argument with warmth and generosity; his wisdom fills these pages. John Wallace introduced me to Highlander Folk School and the importance of asking questions. Others at the University of Minnesota were extremely helpful in the development of this book, especially Mike Baizerman, Jane Plihal, and Rob Shumer.

In Minnesota, I was immersed in a community of learners at the Jane Addams School, with the Citizenship Group, and then in the broader Neighborhood Learning Community. These experiences gave my ideas about the connection between education and civic life a more practical base. It is difficult to write about the genuine relationships that develop through these experiences, but I am grateful to D'Ann Lesch, Nan Kari, Kari Denissen, Kong Her, Gunnar Liden, the Ly family, Derek Johnson, See Moua, and many others for helping me to try to capture this powerful way of learning in community. Perhaps more than anything, it was my time with Mai Lor Thao and the Xiong family that helped me to understand the importance of learning outside the classroom. They have been great teachers.

Another great teacher, Rick Battistoni, fueled my interest in civic education, and provided timely advice and encouragement. I also want to thank Tom King, Hugh Lena, Keith Morton, Jim Tull, and the students and faculty in the Feinstein Institute for Public Service for introducing me to new ways of thinking about community.

John Saltmarsh saw promise in me as a scholar and practitioner, and has helped me become better at both. Chris Caruso's enthusiasm for this project has been very important, especially as he puts these ideas into practice in New York City's after-school programming; Ross Meyer helped me clarify my arguments and our collaboration on student political engagement has been essential; and Liza Pappas and Adam Reich provided many hours of spirited conversations, along with even better friendships.

Ira Harkavy has helped me see the importance of colleges and universities as vehicles for community problem-solving. I learned much from leaders in the field of civic education, especially Cindy Gibson, Carmen Sirianni, and Liz Hollander and the Campus Compact network. Joe Kahne also provided invaluable support and feedback. Lisa Chesnel of SUNY Press saw the value of this project and made it a better book.

At Miami University, Dick Nault, Denny Roberts, Peggy Shaffer, and John Skillings have shown great faith in the power of community engagement for educating the next generation of democratic citizens through the Harry T. Wilks Leadership Institute.

I need to thank many others for encouraging this project at various stages, including Rick Benjamin, Ben Brandzel, Dick Cone, Piyali Dalal, Gail Daneker, Chris Drury, Ian Keith, Jennifer O'Donoghue, Margaret Post, Stephanie Raill, Maggie Struck, and the beloved community activist, Chuck Matthei.

Most of all, I want to thank my family. My parents Nick Sr. and Paula, a politician and a teacher, nurtured my passion for education and democracy and supported me more than I deserve or could repay. As always, Anna Marie and Alison each provided much-needed encouragement.

I owe my greatest debt and thanks to my wife, Aleida Benitez, whose efforts bring the ideas in this book alive in ways my words never could. Our relationship continually encourages, stretches, and inspires me and this work and gives it all greater meaning. Just as I was finishing this book, our daughter Maya Paula arrived, giving us immense hope for the future, a future we want to be part of making a little more democratic.

Chapter One

Introduction
The Ecology of Civic Learning

> Now the change which is coming into our education is the shifting of the center of gravity. It is a change, a revolution, not unlike that introduced by Copernicus when the astronomical center shifted from the earth to the sun.
>
> —John Dewey, *The School and Society*

Education is seen as the only road to a flourishing democracy. We rely on education to prepare citizens for an ongoing commitment to public life. And yet, "American democracy is at risk," according to a new report from the American Political Science Association's first Standing Committee on Civic Education and Engagement, echoing many previous studies on civic participation.[1] Perhaps part of the problem lies in the way we conceptualize education.

"There is a fundamental problem in the progressive theory of education that I think bears scrutiny by those concerned with the politics of education in contemporary America," begins Lawrence Cremin in his 1975 lecture to the John Dewey Society. Cremin, the former dean of Columbia University's Teachers College who has written extensively on the history of American education, defines the problem as "the tendency to focus so exclusively on the potentialities of the school as a lever of social improvements and reform as to ignore the possibilities of other educative institutions."[2] A narrow educational focus still plagues us today, if anything, it has only gotten worse.

Education has become synonymous with schooling. Since the U.S. Department of Education's National Commission on Excellence in Education warned of the deterioration of American education in *A Nation at Risk*

1

in 1983, the crisis in education has become a national priority for people across the ideological spectrum. But it is common for policy makers, educators, parents, and youth to articulate their concerns with the state of our educational system solely in terms of the school. The bipartisan No Child Left Behind federal legislation, for example, set out to improve educational achievement and accountability through the standardization of American schooling.

Efforts to improve civic education among our youngest citizens have also been focused on the classroom. Increasing concern about America's civic health throughout the 1990s culminated in a report entitled *A Nation of Spectators,* issued by the National Commission on Civic Renewal in 1998. The bipartisan commission warned that citizens were becoming apathetic and disengaged from public life and that "in a time that cries out for civic action, we are in danger of becoming a nation of spectators."[3]

In response, an array of reports and initiatives has appeared calling for an increase in the participation of young people in public life. Most proposed interventions, however, have used schools as the primary platform for civic renewal. For example, a diverse group of more than sixty distinguished educational scholars and practitioners convened by the Center for Information and Research on Civic Learning and Engagement (CIRCLE) and the Carnegie Corporation issued *The Civic Mission of Schools* and launched the subsequent Campaign for the Civic Mission of Schools, urging that K–12 schooling become the primary venue for increasing civic education among our nation's youth.[4]

On the surface, this seems to make sense given the time and resources American society devotes to schooling and the social investment we make in schools as instruments for democratic socialization. As *The Civic Mission of Schools* rightly observes, "Schools are the only institutions with the capacity and mandate to reach virtually every person in the country."[5] Yet schools cannot educate in isolation. Equating education with schooling relieves the rest of society from the responsibility of taking part in the education of young people. It also misses the central issue because what happens in schools reflects what happens outside the classroom. Educational successes and failures are mostly the products of communities and families: underachieving schools simply pass along the inequality of resources from families and communities, while high achieving schools pass along family and community privileges.[6] Finally, limiting education to schooling overlooks important assets for improving our educational system and preparing young people to contribute to our democracy—our communities and community institutions.

"Why is it that we have Boards of Education, but they only hire the superintendent of schools?" Lawrence Cremin often asked.[7] He did not mean that boards of education should oversee all aspects of learning in society. He was asking us to imagine what would happen if we broadened our definition of education to reach

> beyond the schools and colleges to the multiplicity of individuals and institutions that educate—parents, peers, siblings, and friends, as well as families, churches, synagogues, libraries, museums, summer camps, benevolent societies, agricultural fairs, settlement houses, factories, radio stations, and television networks.[8]

This insight offers new hope both for academic and civic outcomes. Specifically, this book explores why community matters in educating for democracy.

Protesting a Restricted View

Jane Addams, the founder of Hull House, Chicago's famous settlement house, once described the settlement movement as "a protest against a restricted view of education."[9] This aptly describes the approach to education explored in this book. A more expansive view of education is founded not only in the theory and practice of the settlement movement, but also in the writings of the educational philosopher John Dewey, the experiments with social centers, folk schools, and citizenship schools earlier in the twentieth century, and today's efforts to create community schools, neighborhood learning communities, and engaged colleges and universities.

The three case studies presented in this book illustrate a comprehensive, community-based approach to civic education. Two cases—Hull House and Highlander Folk School—reveal a subterranean tradition of outstanding civic education that is rooted in communities. These cases laid the philosophical and practical groundwork for a third—the Neighborhood Learning Community, a remarkably innovative contemporary example of education for democracy.

My aim is to examine the ideas and practices that define these innovations and explore how they can help us find new ways to address the educational challenges that confront us: the spread of unfettered marketplace (as opposed to democratic) values; decaying inner-city neighborhoods and schools; the loss of local culture in the age of globalization; continued widening inequalities of wealth and power; and the increasing disempowerment of ordinary citizens over the decisions that affect their lives.[10] In this context, perhaps more than ever, looking at the many institutions that educate for democracy is vital.

Throughout our nation's history, education has been linked to the promise of democracy. Yet over the past century the connection between democracy and education has too often been confined to the classroom. While schools are struggling to achieve their academic and civic responsibilities, we are ignoring many untapped resources. This is harmful to education—it puts too much pressure on a single institution. It is also harmful to democracy—it dismisses the role of the many institutions that educate, and overlooks the potential connections between them. In short, we are failing to expand the circle to make communities real partners in educating for democracy.

When this happens, democracy becomes a consumer good or a spectator activity. At its fullest, however, democracy is more than the rule of law, freedom of the press, or a guarantee of the rights of all citizens to vote. Democracy is the work of free citizens. It involves everyday politics where ordinary people are creators, decision-makers, and actors in all aspects of their public life—from their schools and communities to workplaces and government.[11]

While a strong democracy demands active citizens to address these issues, many commentators have chronicled widespread civic disengagement in the American public and sounded the alarm about the precipitous decline in the civic health of our nation, especially among the young. Whether measured by participation in community affairs, voter turnout, trust in institutions or people, the quality of public discourse, or attention to or knowledge of public affairs, Americans appear increasingly disconnected from each other and from public life.[12]

If democratic citizens are educated, not born, as John Dewey noted, then it seems that American society is abdicating the responsibility to nurture the next generation of engaged citizens. Failure to fulfill these responsibilities now has rippling consequences for the very future of democratic practice.

School reform is essential, but schooling alone cannot do the job of educating for democracy. Looking at schooling alone fails to address the complexities and interconnections of public issues of our time. "The American tendency to equate education and schooling and make schools the instrument for satisfying our wants and alleviating our malaise takes attention from our circumstances," writes John Goodlad of the Center for Educational Renewal. "We beat on schools, leaving the contextual circumstances unaddressed."[13] Schools and communities are inexplicably linked: solutions to the problems in each must be addressed by harnessing the many talents in the "ecology of education."[14]

The first principle of ecology is that each living organism has an ongoing and continual relationship with every other element that makes up its environment. Thus, in our ecosystem, there is interdependence and interconnection between the many parts of the whole environment.[15]

Applying the principles of ecology to education begins with the recognition that not only do many institutions provide for educative growth, but also that the different places, people, events, and institutions that provide learning opportunities are related to one another in a potential learning web. Applying the concept of an ecology of education to educating for democracy leads us to suspect that an ecological approach is not only important for individual learning, but that interdependent and interconnected learning networks are also essential for *civic learning*.[16]

As Cynthia Gibson has argued, a more comprehensive approach to civic education acknowledges the strengths and interconnections between various approaches to civic education, including civics knowledge education, service-learning, political action and community change, and youth development.[17]

This involves shifting the center of civic learning toward the many places where the most powerful personal and civic growth takes place—the entire community. When this happens, the community becomes an essential place for learning; it ties education to civic life through collaborative public problem-solving. The institutions of any community—libraries, recreational centers, local businesses, health clinics, as well as institutions of higher education and schools—support people of all ages in the ongoing process of becoming active and democratic citizens. This shifts the focus from a scarcity model of limited resources to the creation of a civic culture with an abundance of civic resources, as Harry Boyte argues. In the simplest terms, an ecological model for civic learning connects education with civic life.[18]

The Obstacles

There are formidable challenges to connecting education with civic life, including deteriorating schools and inner-city neighborhoods, along with declining social capital and political involvement.

Deteriorating Schools

A Nation at Risk put the need for educational reform on the national agenda more than twenty years ago. In the report, the National Commission on Excellence in Education warned that schools had not kept pace with economic or social changes in society. Education, therefore, needed dramatic improvement for America to compete. The report made these claims in straightforward and explosive statements by arguing, for instance, that "the educational foundations of our society are presently being eroded by a rising tide of mediocrity."[19]

The crisis of public schooling was not "discovered" in 1983, but it had an enormous influence in focusing the nation's energies on education.[20] Historian Diane Ravitch, for instance, argues that the condition of the schools was a "chronic, long-term condition rather than a 'crisis.'" *A Nation at Risk*, she said, "woke up the public and stirred a demand for change."[21] Two decades later, the need for educational improvement is taken for granted by people on all sides of the political spectrum; "better education" has become the most common response to problems ranging from preventing AIDS to reducing crime, poverty, and racism, to confronting global competition. It is also seen as a key to revitalizing American democracy.

A similar wake-up call about the state of the nation's schools was issued by Jonathan Kozol's *Savage Inequalities*, a best-selling book on the tragic conditions of America's inner-city schools. More recently, Kozol laments the lack of progress in overcoming segregated and unequal schools in *The Shame of the Nation*.[22] Kozol brought readers inside the "other America" of underfunded, racially segregated, and badly disadvantaged schools. Kozol documents the grossly unequal education of poor children in the United States by telling the stories—backed by data—of disadvantaged children with few educational opportunities.

Deteriorating Inner-City Neighborhoods

Perhaps nothing illustrates the challenge to democracy caused by deteriorating inner-city neighborhoods more than the dramatic images shown to the nation during the tragedy and aftermath of Hurricane Katrina in the summer of 2005. These images illustrate the poverty, racism, and lack of jobs, adequate healthcare, or opportunity for economic advancement in urban areas across the United States. They also provide a human face to coincide with statistics that document America's urban underclass.

Much research has been done to document, understand, and change the cycle of poverty in inner-city American communities, especially since the 1960s War on Poverty. In *The Truly Disadvantaged*, William Julius Wilson writes about the corrosive effects of high-poverty, inner-city neighborhoods on the people living there. In these neighborhoods, Wilson argues, prolonged joblessness has caused a loss of the basic community institutions—including churches, schools, stores, recreation centers, and community centers. The loss of these institutions coincides with the declining sense of community, neighborhood identification, and explicit norms against aberrant behavior—which, when combined, lead to the deterioration of the social and civic organization of inner-city neighborhoods.[23]

Wilson's later work extends to this research by further connecting the cycle of poverty with the loss of jobs in inner-city communities. Wilson argues that the problems of inner-city neighborhoods have been caused by the loss of higher paying, blue-collar jobs in the age of the global, service economy. The lack of jobs, inadequate educational institutions, and continuing racial discrimination facing people of color in inner-city neighborhoods creates a cycle of poverty as well as one of hopelessness.[24]

Declining Social Capital

Documentation of the harsh conditions of inner-city schools and communities has played an important role in making educational reform a national priority. Unfortunately, education reform has too often been narrowly interpreted as school reform. Educational reform, therefore, has seldom been connected with the community. Yet the community is also suffering from the decline of what has been termed "social capital," defined as the social networks and relationships between citizens.

In 1966, sociologist James S. Coleman's study *Equality of Educational Opportunity,* known as "the Coleman Report," made the controversial claim that schools were far less significant than family or community in the lives of children. Coleman found that family and community resources were more important predictors of test score performance than school resources.[25]

Coleman's research builds the foundation for an ecological educational approach that acknowledges the importance of the relationships among the many institutions that educate. His research helped initiate more recent debate about the importance of social capital. Coleman documents the significance of community support and infrastructure for the healthy growth of children and found that children with greater social capital are more successful in school; those with fewer social networks are less successful. Thus, children from inner-city neighborhoods in which community institutions have deteriorated are at a severe disadvantage.[26]

Harvard Professor Robert Putnam called attention to America's declining social capital over the past forty years in his landmark 1995 article, "Bowling Alone."[27] Putnam found that Americans are not joining voluntary associations such as neighborhood clubs, PTAs, fraternal organizations, the Red Cross—or even bowling leagues—as much as they did in the past. As a result, the trust and social networks developed through these associations are declining as Americans literarily and figuratively choose to "bowl alone." In his much-anticipated book, also entitled *Bowling Alone,* Putnam warns that this decline of social networks, norms of reciprocity and trustworthiness, and groups that foster these networks, is dangerous for democracy. He argues, therefore, that civil society must be rebuilt through an increase in interactions and social connections between citizens.[28]

Putnam's work documenting the importance of social capital to American democracy led him to study the connections between social capital and educational achievement. Putnam finds that revitalizing community life may be a *prerequisite* to revitalizing American education. His initial findings indicate, not surprisingly, that family, parent–school, within-school, and community-based social capital has a major influence on the educational process.

In examining comparative statewide educational performance in the United States, Putnam finds a strong correlation between social capital and educational performance—a connection that is even stronger than that between socioeconomic or racial characteristics and educational performance. Putnam argues that rather than blaming teachers, young people, curriculum, or the administration of schools, the actual "culprit for the educational misadventure of American youth over the past several decades may be the civic lethargy and social disengagement of American citizens."[29]

Declining Political Involvement

The crisis for our communities cuts into the very fabric of our democracy. Along with a decrease in social capital, there is also mounting evidence of declining political involvement.[30] The National Commission on Civic Renewal, co-chaired by Sam Nunn and William Bennett, concludes:

> Too many of us have become passive and disengaged. Too many of us lack confidence in our capacity to make basic moral and civic judgments, to join with our neighbors to do the work of community, to make a difference. Never have we had so many opportunities for participation, yet rarely have we felt so powerless. . . . In a time that cries out for civic action, we are in danger of becoming a nation of spectators.[31]

In "a nation of spectators," politics is relegated to experts and political insiders and ordinary people become consumers of public life, rather than productive, engaged citizens. This trend is especially troubling for young people.

For example, the National Association of Secretaries of State's *New Millennium Project*, a study of the political attitudes of fifteen to twenty-four year olds came to the alarming conclusion that "America is in danger of developing a permanent non-voting class." Researchers found that young people lack interest, trust, and knowledge about American politics, politicians, and public life—and are generally cynical about America's future.[32]

Similarly, in *The Vanishing Voter*, Thomas Patterson noted, "Today's young adults are less politically interested and informed than any cohort of young people on record." On study of citizen involvement in presidential elections, Patterson concluded that the period between 1960 and 2000 marks the longest decline in turnout in the nation's history.[33] These trends have been charted by the annual survey of 250,000 college freshmen, conducted by the Higher Education Research Institute (HERI) at the University of California, Los Angeles, since the mid-1960s. In the more than three decades since the initiation of the survey, every significant indicator of political engagement has fallen by at least half. In 2003, the survey reported, for example, that only 26 percent of students entering college expressed an interest in keeping up with political affairs—the lowest level reported since the survey was established in 1966. In that year, student interest in politics was reported at 58 percent.[34]

Reclaiming Education, Community, and Democracy

Overcoming the problems of deteriorating public schools and inner-city neighborhoods, along with declining community bonds and political involvement requires new ways of thinking about the connections between reclaiming education, community, and democracy. A more expansive way of thinking about education for democracy means we must think *comprehensively*, *relationally*, and *publicly*.[35] We must rely on the myriad places where people learn and act collectively; we must emphasize bridging the connections between these formal and informal educational opportunities; and we must promote the public dimensions of education by teaching democratic skills, values, knowledge, and practices. All these ways of thinking and acting are essential for making civic learning a vital part of American education.

The need to pursue civic learning is currently being addressed by a host of initiatives. Most prominently, the Campaign for the Civic Mission of Schools, a coalition of more than forty leading organizations, chaired by former Supreme Court Justice Sandra Day O'Conner and former Colorado Governor Roy Romer, is building on the *Civic Mission of Schools* report to increase the quality of civic learning in America's schools.

In higher education, a host of organizations, networks, and initiatives are attempting to renew the fundamental mission of colleges and universities as "agents of democracy." The term was used by a group of prominent college presidents in the *Presidents' Fourth of July Declaration on the Civic Responsibility of Higher Education*. The July 4, 1999, declaration, which was orchestrated by Campus Compact, a national coalition of more than 1,000 colleges and universities, called on higher education to take seriously its commitment to civic learning and democratic renewal.

Many other networks, initiatives, and practices have become part of a "civic renewal movement in higher education."[36] For example, the American Association of State Colleges and Universities has partnered with the *New York Times* on the "American Democracy Project" at 183 of its member campuses. Civic engagement, in fact, is featured in the strategic agenda of nearly every national higher education association, including the American Council on Education, the American Association of Community Colleges, the Council of Independent Colleges, and an increasing number of disciplinary associations.[37]

Education in the Community

There are many promising models for reclaiming democracy, community, and education through "civic renewal movements." In *Civic Innovation in America,* Carmen Sirianni and Lewis Friedland highlight innovative models in the areas of community organizing, public health care, the environment, and journalism. Lisbeth Schorr's *Common Purpose* presents comprehensive, long-term models that effectively address poverty and the growing underclass, and include lessons for scaling up and reforming public institutions. Harry Boyte and Nancy Kari, in *Building America,* find promise in the concept of "public work" and cite many hopeful historical and contemporary examples in government, nonprofits, higher education, and low-income communities. More recently, Boyte documents how the Center for Democracy and Citizenship is helping to catalyze everyday politics in neighborhoods, schools, community institutions, and institutions of higher education. Finally, Peter Levine describes the growth of a "reasonably tight and robust network" for civic renewal movement in such fields as democratic community organizing, community economic development, deliberative democracy practices, public media, service-learning, and civic education.[38]

This book focuses on the importance of community in these civic efforts. Jerome Stein, the director of the Project on Youth and Community at the University of Minnesota, contends that "education in the community" is not a fad or simply an academic curiosity; rather, "it is a new field of human endeavor."[39] This field is an essential component of educating for democracy.

Education in the community is active learning that takes place outside of, but often connected with, the classroom. It involves more than a one-time community service project; it means intentionally putting education in the context of long-term community-building efforts. It is most often place-based, using a collaborative, integrated, problem-solving approach.[40]

Education in the community represents a particular way of connecting the many places in which people learn and act collectively; it signifies a way of educating that calls on democratic community building practices, and it utilizes nonprofessional expertise. Like the lessons on the importance of local customs and wisdom from James Scott's study of the failure of centralized approaches, education in the community gives an "indispensable role to practical knowledge, informal processes, and improvisation in the face of unpredictability."[41] This approach, as we will see, can also help leverage the diverse ways citizens act for positive change in communities. In short, education in the community can serve as a foundation not only for meaningful learning, but also for a vibrant democracy.

It seems clear that we learn from family, friends, neighbors, and youth workers as well as teachers; that we learn in libraries, community centers, youth groups, and more informal places like hair salons, pizzerias, basketball courts, soccer fields, hip-hop circles, and neighborhood parks, as well as in schools, colleges, and universities. Within the framework of education in the community, these places of learning are not disconnected. This approach advocates partnering, for example, schools with families, neighbors with community-based organizations, and colleges and universities with religious, cultural, and business groups.

Critics have often raised questions about the lack of capacity for such collaborations. While some community institutions work to support the schools—taking on fund-raising tasks, tutoring responsibilities, or even advocating for policy changes—most existing collaborations seldom have a shared vision for success. School officials are often unaware of the goals (or activities) of families and communities, and community partners are often unaware of how their work can connect with learning outcomes.[42]

In an era of high-stakes testing in underresourced schools, there is also concern that community education efforts load additional responsibilities onto already burdened educators. This need not be the case. Education in the community recognizes the abundance of resources for learning, creating common efforts that creatively tap the many assets for civic learning. "In that way," Ira Harkavy and Marty Blank write, "schools will no longer be isolated, and entire communities can be engaged in the most vital work of a vibrant democracy: the full education of all its children."[43]

The case studies in this book reveal that intergenerational, holistic, and interconnected education that deliberately connects community learning with civic engagement is an effective strategy for civic renewal. It has been a strategy used successfully within the social settlement, social center, labor, civil rights, community schools, and service-learning movements.

Civic Learning Models

According to Peter Levine, director of CIRCLE and a primary architect of the movement for civic renewal, civic learning might best be defined by the list of goals set out by *The Civic Mission of Schools* for competent and responsible citizens. These four interrelated objectives include the aims that young people

- are informed and thoughtful; have a grasp and an appreciation of history and fundamental processes of American democracy; have an understanding and awareness of public and community issues; and have the ability to obtain information, think critically, and enter into dialogue among others with different perspectives.
- participate in their communities through membership in or contributions to organizations working to address an array of cultural, social, political, and religious interests and beliefs.
- act politically by having the skills, knowledge, and commitment needed to accomplish public purposes, such as group problem solving, public speaking, petitioning and protesting, and voting.
- have moral and civic virtues such as concern for the rights and welfare of others, social responsibility, tolerance and respect, and belief in the capacity to make a difference.[44]

Perhaps the most succinct definition of civic learning comes from John Saltmarsh, who writes that "civic learning is rooted in respect for community-based knowledge, grounded in experiential and reflective modes of teaching and learning, aimed at active participation in American democracy, and aligned with institutional change efforts to improve student learning."[45]

Developing civic pathways to increase these values, skills, knowledge, and practices is the work of many policy makers, educators, and foundations, as evidenced by initiatives to increase civic engagement among our nation's youth. The models of civic learning presented in this book are part of an effort to create new ideas, metaphors, and practices for approaches to education. As Theodore Sizer writes:

> The traditional ways of perceiving adolescents' learning must be held in check, the governing metaphors and familiar practices diligently challenged, and no idea peremptorily dismissed because of its presumed impracticality or perceived ideological roots; all must be addressed at once.[46]

This approach distinguishes between school-centered learning, the traditional model in which the school is the central hub for education, and education that recognizes the many places where people learn and their connections to each other, termed "education in the community." It represents the shifting center of gravity that takes place when community and community institutions are essential pieces in the educational system (see Figure 1.1).

Figure 1.1 Approaches to Education: Schooling and the Community

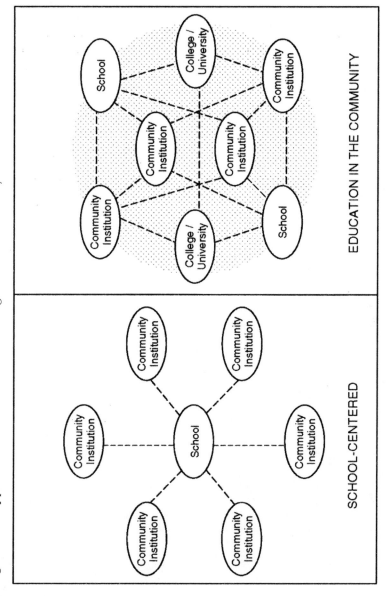

Considerable research has been conducted on various conceptions of civic engagement.[47] In the most extensive cross-generational study, a research team funded by the Pew Charitable Trusts organizes the many ways that people are involved in public life into nineteen indicators that fit into three broad categories: civic activities, electoral activities, and political voice. The survey that led to *The Civic and Political Health of the Nation* measures civic activities in three ways: by organized volunteer activity focused on solving problems and helping others; by electoral activities such as voting and election-related work; and by political voice— activities that people engage in to give expression to their political and social viewpoints.[48]

I define civic engagement as *public work* (projects creating things of public value); *community involvement* (membership in community groups and community service); *community organizing* (canvassing, protesting, and building power relations); *civic knowledge* (awareness of government processes and following public affairs); *conventional political action* (voting, campaign work, and advocacy for legislation); and *public dialogue* (deliberative conversations on public issues). These overlapping and interconnected civic practices are depicted in Figure 1.2.

Figure 1.3 represents the approaches to educating for democracy revealed in the studies presented in this book, with models that connect education in the community and civic engagement. As Figure 1.3 illustrates, not all education in the community connects with civic engagement. For example, learning in sports, summer camps, and even many collaborative projects between schools and communities provides educative growth, but these are not necessarily examples of public work, community organizing, public dialogue, civic knowledge, conventional political action, or even community involvement.

At the same time, many examples of civic engagement have no connection to education in the community. For instance, classroom-based social studies can provide civic knowledge, a letter writing campaign to a local official is a good example of conventional political action, and young people on a debate team participate in public dialogues, but none of these activities necessarily involves learning in the context of the broader community.

Deliberate, holistic, integrated, and public approaches to learning-in-action are features of the model of education for democracy in this book. Hull House, Highlander Folk School, and the Neighborhood Learning Community are important and powerful cases because each employs a broader ecology of civic learning. This model serves as the foundation for a new way to think about civic education.

Figure 1.2   Civic Engagement

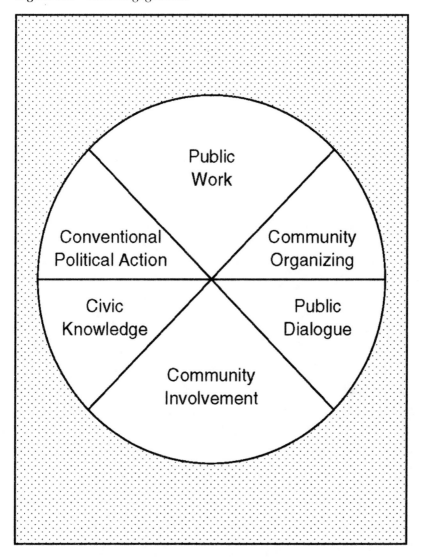

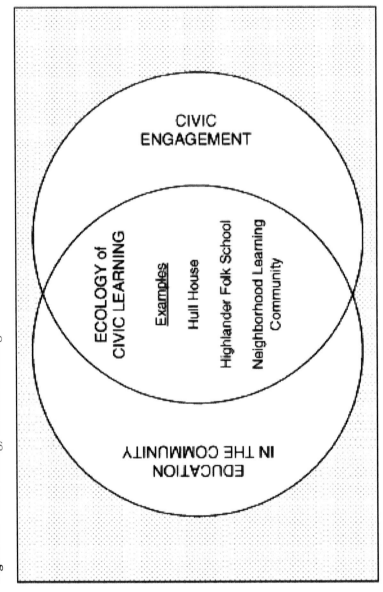

Figure 1.3   The Ecology of Civic Learning

A Different Kind of Politics

The ecological approach to civic learning suggests that community engagement is an essential pathway for civic renewal. Of course, like schooling, the community alone is no panacea. Nevertheless, many opportunities exist to bring us back into educative balance by focusing on community assets, working toward public outcomes, and making education a more expansive endeavor. Addressing these issues is essential to rethinking civic education. The ecological approach also represents the framework within which we can educate for a different type of politics—one that moves us beyond the narrow interests of a scarcity model.

Research on youth organizations in the community seems to support the role of community revitalization in political revitalization. Stanford professor Milbrey McLaughlin connects community-based learning with positive outcomes for youth. In *Community Counts*, McLaughlin finds that focusing on community is a proven strategy for the personal, social, and civic growth of young people. McLaughlin's study, sponsored by the Spencer Foundation, reports that community-based organizations can make a powerful and positive contribution to the lives of young people. In these organizations, young people engage in positive activities, build caring relationships, gain self-confidence, and develop ambitious career aspirations. Influenced by their involvement in the community, these young people gain essential civic characteristics, as they "intend to be assets to their communities and examples for others to follow."[49] Perhaps more important, young people involved in community organizations have a higher rate of civic engagement and a greater commitment to getting involved.

While researchers are finding a decline in political and civic involvement, there is surging interest in, and opportunities for, community involvement by young people in community service and service-learning.[50] For instance, according to the Higher Education Research Institute (HERI), an all-time high of 83.2 percent of the freshman entering class of 2005 report that they volunteered at least occasionally during their senior year in high school, and 70.6 percent report that they typically volunteered on a weekly basis.[51]

Although these activities have been of significant interest to scholars and policy makers interested in the health of American democracy, many have since found that community service has limitations for increasing political engagement. Community service, they argue, is based on apolitical notions of volunteerism wherein too few efforts are made to link involvement in community with notions of power.[52] Students therefore tend to believe that engagement with the political process is unimportant and irrelevant for change and that community service is a more effective way to solve public problems. They often see community service as an *alternative to* politics.

Many critics observe that an emphasis on "serving needs" illustrates an approach in which people with privilege or professional expertise act as "charitable helpers," not reciprocal partners in community renewal. This disempowering approach often hides the power issues among volunteers, nonprofit professionals, and the people they "serve." One of the most vocal critics of this approach, John McKnight, points out the role community service plays in creating an industry of professionals whose very jobs rely on the continued existence of community deficiencies—and who tend to see people they serve in terms of their deficits, rather than their assets.[53]

Service can also fail to recognize the nature of politics and power. Harry Boyte contends that service routinely "neglects to teach about root causes and power relationships, fails to stress productive impact, ignores politics, and downplays the strengths and talents of those being served." Boyte also points out that service "does not teach the political skills that are needed to work effectively toward solving society's problems: public judgment, the collaborative exercise of power, conflict resolution, negotiating, bargaining, and holding others accountable."[54]

And while it was assumed that service-learning programs would lead to greater political participation, the evidence for this is unclear.[55] David Mathews, president of the Kettering Foundation, one of the leading voices for democratic renewal writes, "Service programs, although filled with political implications that bright students are likely to recognize, tend to be kept carefully distanced from political education." It is, therefore, "difficult to say what effect, if any, these service programs have on civic education."[56]

And yet, there is a growing movement among young people in the public work tradition, which begins to define a different kind of politics that enables students to find participatory, inclusive, open, creative, and deliberative ways of addressing public problems. For instance, in 2001, thirty-three college students met at the Wingspread Conference Center in Racine, Wisconsin, to discuss their "civic experiences" in higher education.

This conversation led to the student-written *New Student Politics*, which forcefully argues that student work in communities is not an alternative to politics, but rather an "alternative politics." The students at Wingspread noted that they see democracy as richly participatory; that negotiating differences is a key element of politics; that their service in communities was done in the context of systemic change; and that higher education needs to do more to promote civic education.[57]

Furthermore, the students proclaimed, "We see ourselves as misunderstood by those who measure student engagement by conventional standards that don't always fit our conceptions of democratic participation." *The New Student Politics* concludes by quoting E. J. Dionne's analysis that "the great reforming generations are the ones that marry the aspirations of service to the possibilities of politics and harness the good work done in local communities to transform a nation." The students, it seems, are part of a long tradition of younger generations casting a new civic identity and new way of thinking and acting for the public good.[58]

This "new student politics," writes Harry Boyte, is a "sign that today's students in American colleges and universities are beginning to think and act politically, as organizers for change."[59] A series of public declarations and national campaigns on college campuses further illustrate this. Following up on the Wingspread Conference, for example, Campus Compact launched a national campaign aimed at involving college students in public life, called *Raise Your Voice*. Since 2002, students on more than 300 college campuses have been involved in mapping civic assets on campuses, hosting dialogues on public issues on campuses and in communities, and organizing for social change.[60]

The insights derived from these innovative efforts have made for good scholarship and ring true to professionals in the field, and, more important, to ordinary citizens. Unfortunately, they have had little impact on education policy. Stifled by the technocratic impulse that narrows democratic possibilities, education policy is still school-based and expert driven. The prominent educator and champion of small schools, Theodore Sizer, acknowledged this lack of public impact in his memoir, *The Red Pencil*.

Sizer recognizes the potential for the ecology of education on educational policy. Drawing on his fifty years of experience in education and on lessons learned from his former teacher, Lawrence Cremin, Sizer writes, "Educators should accept Cremin's challenge and move toward the design of modern ways to educate youth—a very rethinking of deliberate education, rethinking that includes, but goes substantially beyond, the good things that can happen in the familiar building."[61]

The cacophony of voices calling for new ways of thinking comes from those outside of the field of education as well. For instance, organizational system-thinker Peter Senge says in *Community Youth Development Journal*, "Until we go back to thinking about school as the totality of the environment in which a child grows up, we can expect no deep changes. Change requires a community—people living and working together, assuming some common responsibility for something that's of deep concern and interest to all of them, their children."[62]

These observations are just as salient for civic education. But change will not occur because "it is the right thing to do." As I contend in the conclusion of this book, it requires a different kind of politics. Similarly, Harry Boyte argues, "We need bold, savvy, and above all *political* citizens and civic institutions if we are to tame a technological, manipulative state, to transform an increasingly materialistic and competitive culture, and to address effectively the mounting practical challenges of a turbulent and interconnected world."[63]

One strategy for implementing the ecology of civic learning is simply telling the stories that run counter to the dominant narrative. In this book, I attempt to make a small contribution toward this effort.

Overview

In chapter two, John Dewey's speech on "The School as a Social Centre" serves as an anchor for a review of the history and practices of "education writ large." This chapter identifies significant historical developments for education in the community, including social centers, community schools, and engaged colleges and universities. I also introduce innovative ideas and practices, and the significant people, such as Leonard Covello, Elsie Clapp, and Ernest Boyer, who pioneered these movements.

The next three chapters present the case studies: Hull House, Highlander Folk School, and the Neighborhood Learning Community. In the Hull House case study in chapter three, I examine the efforts of Jane Addams and her experiment with democracy in an urban, immigrant neighborhood at the turn of the twentieth century. Though she never used the language of "civic learning," Jane Addams serves as one of its earliest advocates and practitioners. In this chapter, I consider the influences, people, and ideas that shaped the Hull House programs and educational approach. I also explore the Labor Museum, Hull House's intergenerational democratic experiment in which new immigrants attempted to use education as a force for social and political change.

In chapter four I examine the democratic education practiced by Myles Horton, Septima Clark, Bernice Robinson, and others at Highlander Folk School, along with how this effort was partially inspired by Jane Addams and Hull House. I explore Highlander's founding, educational philosophy, and practices, and detail the most successful civic learning program implemented by Highlander: the Citizenship Schools, which emerged as key civic educational projects during the civil rights movement of the 1950 and 1960s.

In chapter five I examine a contemporary case study, the Neighborhood Learning Community in St. Paul, Minnesota. The Neighborhood

Learning Community builds upon the lessons of Hull House and Highlander, but also gives new meaning to the ecology of civic learning through its efforts to connect multiple institutions in a learning network in an urban community. This case study illustrates the power of community-based initiatives and public practices as well as the importance of establishing an intentional educational network whose job is to connect education in the community with civic engagement. The chapter concludes with obstacles to and successful examples of school–community collaborations.

Chapter six includes an examination of the democratic habits of community practitioners, including "thinking-in-action," connecting diverse communities, and using informal education. The chapter also describes essential democratic skills and tools, such as community asset mapping, community power mapping, and "being local," for promoting civic education.

The key lessons learned from analysis of the case studies in this book are outlined in chapter seven. The chapter concludes with policy recommendations, the rationales for change, and a road map for future explorations of civic education.

Readers who are concerned by current trends toward civic disengagement, especially among the young, and a lack of ideas about how education can play a role in civic renewal will find much to be hopeful about in the pages that follow. It is not my intention to provide the whole story—or the last word—on the ecology of civic learning. That is overly ambitious. What I set out to do is introduce new ways of thinking about civic education and to describe imaginative educational practices that will shift the center of education, open up new possibilities, and widen the conversation on the connections among education, community, and democracy.

Chapter Two

Education Writ Large

So education has a new scope and a new task. If democracy is thus really to rethink itself to the new cooperative endeavor, a new education must arise, partly to include all citizens in a new type of adult education, partly to remake the schools and other educative institutions so that more effectual social thinking and action will result. Education is here conceived as a function of many institutions in the community, the church, the club, the school, and all other social organizations with a program of public or semipublic activities.

—William Kilpatrick, *Youth Serves the Community*

Schools as Social Centers

In order to better understand the ecology of civic learning, certain developments in the history and research on education in the community and civic engagement need to be explored. As a general introduction that will anchor the entire history of expansive models of education, one must look to an influential speech delivered by John Dewey in July 1902. Dewey remarked:

We may say that the conception of the school as a social centre is born of our entire democratic movement. Everywhere we see signs of the growing recognition that the community owes to each one of its members the fullest opportunity for development. Everywhere we see the growing recognition that the community life is defective and distorted excepting as it does thus care for all its constituent parts. This is no longer viewed as a matter of charity, but as a matter of justice—nay, even of something higher and better than justice—a necessary phase of developing and growing life.[1]

When he spoke these words in Minneapolis, Minnesota, to the National Council of Education, John Dewey developed a theoretical foundation for why schools must see their roles as connected to communities. In the speech entitled "The School as a Social Centre," Dewey asserts, "our community life has awakened" and argues that changes in society at the turn of the twentieth century required a new educational approach. As part of a broader conception of citizenship, Dewey concludes that schools must act as social centers by connecting their educational missions with the surrounding community.[2]

Dewey, at this time on the board of Hull House and a close friend of Jane Addams, frequently cites settlement houses, and specifically Hull House, as the model for the role schools should play in society. The "widened and enlightened education" Dewey saw as necessary was provided outside the schools in the settlements. Dewey finds that diverse relations are important to education and observes that in the settlements "there is mixing of people up with each other." He then adds that these conditions, "promote their getting acquainted with the best side of each other."[3]

"Dewey's notion of 'the school as a social center' reflected the vision of Addams and other settlement workers that urban public schools would incorporate settlement ideas and functions," write Ira Harkavy and John Puckett. "The school and the curriculum would become, in effect, focal points of neighborhood development, improvement, and stabilization."[4] Dewey boldly concludes his speech by declaring that every public school should take the approach proven so effective by the settlements.

The 1902 speech was a very significant event. It occurred at a time of rapid industrialization and urbanization, as well as a period that saw an increase in non–English-speaking immigrants that changed the fabric of American civic and community life. Although Dewey was known primarily for his writings about schooling and democracy, these new times required a new approach. With Dewey's voice serving as a catalyst, education in the community took a new life and focus at the turn of the twentieth century.

This speech marked the beginning of a movement out of which came an array of educational activities—formal and informal—within and between communities, colleges and universities, and schools. Over the past century, education in the community has developed a solid foundation with models such as community schools, settlement houses, community learning centers, folk schools, social centers, recreation centers, Catholic Worker houses, community arts and theater, internships, alternatives schools, and the pedagogy of service-learning.[5]

Today, more than 100 years later, the ideas Dewey set forth could not be more relevant. In this chapter, I provide a review of where Dewey's ideas have taken us, exploring what Ellen Lagemann has wonderfully termed "education writ large" through an examination of the historic landscape that proceeds what I am terming the ecology of civic learning.[6]

Dewey's 1902 "School as a Social Centre" speech helped articulate the emergence of education in the community, which took many forms. As previously noted, education in the community might include, specifically, learning that occurs in social settlement houses, urban playgrounds, vacation schools and after-school programs, social centers, folk schools, libraries, public art, museums, internships, and community schools.[7] Dewey contributed greatly to the theory and practice of many of these movements. He founded the Laboratory School based on the ideas of experiential education in Chicago with his wife Alice in 1896, wrote extensively on the philosophy of education for democracy, contributed to models of community schools, served as a foundation for the ideas of engaged colleges and universities, and articulated a more expansive view of education, especially in his later writings. Dewey came to view education as more than schooling, an embodiment of the idea that "all life is educative."[8]

In addition, Dewey's students spearheaded many of the most influential educational reform efforts over the past century. Joseph K. Hart, for example, forcefully pursued the ideas and practices of the ecology of civic learning. One of the earliest board members of the Highlander Folk School, Hart wrote one book entitled *Education in the Humane Community*.[9] Elsewhere, in arguing for the importance of building educative communities for democracy, Hart states:

> Education is not apart from life. . . . The democratic problem in education is not primarily a problem of training children; it is a problem of *making a community* within which children cannot help growing up to be democratic, intelligent, disciplined to freedom, reverent of the goods of life, and eager to share in the tasks of the age. Schools cannot produce the result; nothing but the community can do so.[10]

Hart concludes that schools can *only* be the hope of democracy if they "learn how to discover the intelligence latent in the community."[11]

The social center movement, recreation movement, community schools, and engaged colleges and universities are some of the educational influences in the twentieth century that attempted to discover the "intelligence latent in the community."[12]

Social Centers

The first social center is believed to have emerged at Speyer School Settlement, an experimental school established by Columbia Teachers College in 1902. It began, partly, out of the desire to make "wider use of school facilities."[13] As social centers, schools could become places for educational extension, adult education, neighborhood meetings, and community discussions. The "wider use" justification was proposed initially on the grounds of efficiency. Charles Eliot, then president of Harvard, made this argument in 1903 by drawing out a cost-benefit analysis of the schools. "The present inadequate use of the schoolhouse is wasteful precisely in proportion to the costliness of the grounds and buildings," Eliot argued.[14]

With an economic as well as democratic basis, social centers had a period of rapid expansion in the early twentieth century. In his excellent book on civic activism during the Progressive Era, *Creating a Democratic Public*, Kevin Mattson describes the democratic vibrancy of the social center movement. The social centers, according to Mattson, taught civic skills, like deliberation and debate, along with civic values, like inclusion and fairness. "Social centers taught participants that any citizen—not just intellectuals—could deliberate and debate," Mattson writes. "Citizens learned that they themselves could create a deliberating, democratic public."[15]

Rochester developed an impressive social center movement led by Edward J. Ward, who was also influenced by John Dewey, Jane Addams, and the settlement house movement. However, Ward was also determined to overcome the disempowering "charitable uplift" aspects he saw in settlement houses. He felt this could be done on two grounds. First, the social center movement grew from the demand of the community—not on reformers moving into a new and foreign neighborhood. Second, the social center movement was supported by public funds, not individual charity. One journalist observed that through the social centers, "it is being discovered that neither charity nor 'uplift' will meet the fundamental difficulties [of social life]. Neither is democratic."[16]

Rochester city government and the Board of Education provided funds for the activities as the result of an effective lobbying campaign by several civic groups. Most important, these funds gave community members themselves governing power. This meant that local communities petitioned the school board to open social centers and then determined the topics of discussion. The sole requirement was attendance, with a minimum requirement of twenty-five participants. The Rochester experiment also used the schools as public space for polling locations, meetings of civic groups and school officials, speeches, forums, and community programs.

The issues discussed illustrate that the social center movement connected community learning with politics. The public dialogues ranged from local issues, like where streetcar tracks should be placed, and local housing conditions, to national issues, such as immigration. Political candidates and elected officials were also regularly invited to speak on these issues to—what had become—a more informed citizenry.

While significant, the experiment in Rochester was short-lived. In 1910, funds were cut because the entrenched political bosses feared the open, democratic dialogues the centers were cultivating. Nevertheless, the social center idea would live on. Ward brought the idea with him to the University of Wisconsin where social centers again flourished throughout Wisconsin. One of the strongest examples was in Milwaukee where in 1912 nearly one-fourth of the neighborhood schools had neighborhood civic clubs. The social center idea also spread nationally. By 1912, 101 cities carried on social center work in 338 school buildings throughout the country prior to a loss of focus on these types of civic experiments with the advent of World War I.[17]

The legacy of social centers is perhaps best captured in their ability to create institutions in which ordinary citizens could learn the arts of democracy. Social center activists, like the civic leaders in the following chapters, believed that "education could no longer be thought of as cloistered in formal institutions of learning."[18] Activists at the time argued that the movement was an example of a "broader conception of education."[19] Believing that the school was too abstract and undemocratic, one observer noted, by contrast, that the social centers connected learning with civic engagement in that they were "educational in the sense that where there is human aspiration and joint effort for better things there is education."[20]

The social centers provide a practical model for connecting democracy and education. "Advocates for the school as a social center movement seem to have believed deeply in the equivalence of democracy and education," writes Jerome Stein. "What was democratic was educational, and what was educational was democratic."[21]

Playgrounds, Vacation Schools, and Recreation Centers

At the same time, connected movements for public playgrounds, vacation schools, and recreations centers were taking place. The playground movement began in the United States in 1886 in Boston when piles of sand were left in churchyards for children to play in. This led to the creation of the first public playground in Chicago in 1893, initiated by Hull

House. Settlement workers around the country carried this agenda forward through the creation of the National Playground Association in 1906 and soon playgrounds were linked with neighborhood schools.

Similarly, activity-oriented vacation schools, which included play, field trips, nature study, and storytelling, formed in the 1890s in New York City and Boston and became linked with the public schools. Soon recreation centers were opened in New York City and by 1910 recreation centers appeared in almost two dozen cities; by 1917, there were thousands of recreation centers in cities across the United States. This increase led to the creation of the Playground and Recreation Association of America in 1912 to advocate for increased opportunities for free, public spaces.[22]

The social center movement and the recreation movement were both important precursors to the community school movement. These developments also grew into modern community centers. In fact, social centers became known as community centers around 1915 and by 1930 New York City alone had almost 500 community centers with an attendance of over four million people annually.[23] Today, thanks to these efforts, community centers, recreation centers, and public playgrounds have become taken-for-granted parts of neighborhood life that serve as underpinnings for learning and collective action in communities.

Community Schools

An early definition of a community school by the National Society for the Study of Education defines community schools by their dual, interrelated educational functions. A community school is: "A school that has two distinctive emphasis—service to the entire community, not merely to the children of school age; and discovery, development, and use of the resources of the community as part of the educational facilities of the school."[24] These dual roles are seen throughout the many inventions and reinventions of community schooling.

Henry Barnard

One of the earliest publications describing the role of schools in the broader community was written by the first commissioner of education in the United States, Henry Barnard. Barnard's *Report of the Conditions and Improvements of the Public Schools of Rhode Island,* submitted in 1845 while he was school commissioner of Rhode Island, described the role of the school in improving community life.[25] After visiting every town in the state twice, Barnard presented a comprehensive series of recommendations to the state legislature for improving the educational system in Rhode Island. Barnard calls for communities to provide public libraries in each town. He discusses the importance of parent involvement in education. He recommends that school learning be experiential and "deal less with books and deal more with real objects in nature around." For example, "the elementary principles of botany, mineralogy, geology, and chemistry" should be taught through "their connection with practical agriculture."[26]

Barnard includes suggestions on school attendance policies, teacher preparation, and the construction of school houses, and also argues that schools in manufacturing districts should include halls for popular lectures, and space for evening classes, reading circles, a library, and gatherings of conversations on the issues of the day. Public education was the key to overcoming class divisions. To this aim, Barnard felt, good schools must work with other supplemental means—including community and religious institutions—to improve the conditions of the poor because "all these things will do good and tend to educate the whole community, and improve the condition of the manufacturing population."[27]

Schools of Tomorrow

Some of the earliest writing on applications of the community school idea, not surprisingly, appeared in *Schools of Tomorrow* in 1915. Writing with his daughter Evelyn, Dewey highlights examples of schools acting as social centers in Gary and Indianapolis, Indiana; he argues, more radically, that these schools should serve as models for public education. Dewey writes, "Every community has the right to expect and demand that schools supported at public expense for public ends shall serve community uses as widely as possible."[28]

In order to serve the community in Gary, Indiana, school facilities were open all day, evenings, and Saturdays. Buildings had a gymnasium, pool, and playground for community use. The local community was an integral part of the curriculum and the schools attempted to make learning reciprocal by having the school serve as a resource for the community. The Deweys also realized the importance of putting the entire community to good use for students: "In discipline, in social life, and in curriculum the Gary schools are doing everything possible, in cooperation with church and home, to use to the best educational purpose every resource of money, organization and neighborhood influence."[29]

In another chapter, the Deweys describe P.S. 26, located in one of the poorest neighborhoods in Indianapolis, as "a social settlement for the neighborhood." However, like the contemporary authors of *The Civic Mission of Schools*, the Deweys recognized the importance of the public dimensions of schooling.[30] A school that played the role of a settlement in the neighborhood had a decided advantage over the traditional settlement—namely, its reach. Dewey recognized that the school "comes in contact with all the children living within its district for a number of hours each day, while settlements reach the children for only a few scattered hours each week."[31] In comparing P.S. 26 with the settlements, Dewey concludes that the school has a larger influence because it is not an act of charity by those who are financially well-off; rather, the school is a public institution, financed by the public, and thus "owned by the people."

Elsie Clapp

John Dewey's impact on community schools is not only seen in his writing, but also through his students. A too seldom referenced pioneer for community schools is Elsie Clapp, a student of Dewey's who took at least fourteen courses from Dewey at Columbia University and Teachers College from 1907 to 1912. Clapp was also Dewey's graduate assistant for twelve courses between 1911 and 1927. Dewey recommended that Clapp replace him in teaching his education courses at Teachers College upon his retirement in 1927, but she was not appointed.[32] Instead, Clapp applied the ideas from her years with Dewey through the founding of two community schools. Clapp founded and directed the Roger Clark Ballard Memorial School in Jefferson Country, Kentucky, from 1929 to 1934, and then the Arthurdale School and Community Activities in Arthurdale, West Virginia, from 1934 to 1936.

This experience fueled her continued academic work on community–school collaborations. Clapp edited *Progressive Education* from 1937 to 1939; authored *Community Schools in Action*, a pioneering work that draws on the experiences founding and directing these two community schools; and wrote *The Use of Resources in Education*, which argues for the importance of using the entire community as an educational resource.[33]

"It was in Kentucky that we came to an understanding of the nature and function of a community school," Clapp writes. "In Arthurdale, West Virginia, we built a community school and used it as an agency for community education."[34] This "agency for community education" was built in partnership with the local community. There was no separation between school and community life: parents were considered teachers, and teachers were seen as neighbors. "A community school is made *with* the people whose school it is," Clapp wrote. "In the making, teachers lead as fellow-workers. As members themselves of the community, they are citizens as well as teachers, sharing common problems and interests."[35]

At Arthurdale, adult education went on throughout the day and in the evenings. Intergenerational activities of the school included shared work on the homestead, as well as health programs, classes for women on gardening and raising chickens, singing groups, music lessons, an adult drama group, athletics, square dancing, and library training. Community efforts led to the creation of a library for adults and youth, a community garden to grow school lunches, and a health clinic to introduce healthy living, clinical service, and nutritional information.

The lessons for Clapp from her experiences in Kentucky and Arthurdale reveal the importance of flexibility, responding to community needs, and utilizing community assets. Clapp concludes:

> Above all, it seems to me, the record should make clear that in community education one is never dealing with a fixed plan, a formula, or a ready-made organization, but with needs as they are revealed—needs and aspirations of people with all their potentialities and prejudices, their ambitions and handicaps, their ways of thinking and feeling, their patterns of behavior, their relationships and social environment, their cultural and racial background, as well as their physical surroundings.[36]

Dewey realized the importance of the work Clapp was undertaking in making use of the community for learning. In a letter to Clapp, he wrote, "I feel more and more strongly and largely because of your own work that the next educational step or the completion of the one started depends upon educators grasping the significance of their own communities for educational purposes."[37]

Leonard Covello

Clapp and Dewey were not alone in seeing the importance of community for educational purposes. In the 1930s, the Committee on the Community School hoped to intertwine the theory and practice of community-based education by highlighting diverse perspectives and programs in *The Community School.* Committee members, including Myles Horton and William Kilpatrick, another protégé of John Dewey, wrote chapters describing comprehensive educational programs. Samuel Everett sums up the lessons from this early book on the theory and practice of education in the community when he writes: "The authors of this study not only accept the concept that 'all life is educative' but also are helping to organize their communities so that all social agencies are exerting their educational function in cooperating with the schools. The community is actually becoming the school."[38]

The community was certainly becoming the school in New York City under the leadership of Leonard Covello, principal of Benjamin Franklin High School, another of the book's authors. At the same time that Elsie Clapp was developing a rural community school in Arthurdale, Covello was implementing a community school of his own in the urban neighborhood of East Harlem.[39]

Being an Italian immigrant gave Covello empathy for his immigrant students' experiences living between divergent cultures and thus to put an emphasis on validating students' home cultures and communities. It also enabled him to see the value of holistic education. Covello made it a priority that he and his teachers connect with students' families. For instance, like an early settlement worker, Covello lived in the same neighborhood as his school and his students. He thought this was important so that he could see his students and their families in the streets and visit their homes.

Covello's aim for the school–community relationship was reciprocity based on mutual respect, trust, and responsiveness. To accomplish this, every effort was made to nurture learning in the school and in the community. "The community is ordinarily quite ready to respect the school," Covello wrote. "The school, in turn, must give to the community recognition of its importance, must accord a due measure of appreciation of human values that are basically more important than the school itself."[40]

There are many examples of this reciprocal approach in practice. For instance, in the 1930s, the Benjamin Franklin School's PTA and Community Advisory Council led an effort to obtain rent-free use of storefront property near the school, termed "street units." After the property was donated, community members and students worked to fix it up and make it a space for community learning. People donated furniture, a piano, desks, and chairs.

Out of these storefronts came a community library with books in people's native languages, a meeting space for the Friends and Neighbors Club, singing and musical groups, and adult learning centers. Covello, who realized the importance of having this space outside the school, writes:

> We soon discovered that people who would never dream of going near the school, feeling self-conscious, would make use of the facilities of the store fronts—making us further realize the need for small social and educational centers scattered around a neighborhood to supplement the work of the main building in community education.[41]

The work done at Benjamin Franklin High School is an early example of a school connecting learning in the community with civic engagement. Covello's students and staff partnered with parents and community members on projects that made public contributions. Students engaged in community mapping, conducted community research, and utilized community photography.

Covello's autobiography, *The Heart Is the Teacher*, describes some of the innovative curriculum used at Benjamin Franklin High School. The following description of learning done in the 1930s illustrates what may be the first community mapping done by youth, a technique developed further in the 1990s by John McKnight and John Kretzmann that is a central skill for promoting civic learning. Covello writes:

> Social-study classes stressed the theme "Know Your Community!"
>
> The Art Department worked out a huge map of East Harlem, carefully outlining individual blocks. From this original which hung in my office, duplicates of a smaller size were printed and distributed to the various departments of the school and civic organizations of the neighborhoods, to be used for their own purposes.
>
> Slowly, on the master map, we began to accumulate information which, in turn, was fed out to the smaller maps. Before anything else, we wanted to know where our students lived. In varying colors to indicate nationality, we spotted them in the map and were astonished to find distributions and concentrations of population never before realized. As part of their social studies experience, the boys took to the streets after hours with pencil and paper to gather statistical information about their neighborhood which the Art Department, in terms of symbols, transferred to the master map. . . .
>
> It was both significant and depressing, both to the students and to us as teachers, to realize that a community which could support forty-one religious institutions and twenty-two political clubs and one hundred fifty-six bars could boast only a few open playgrounds for its children, three public halls, and no neighborhood newspaper at all.[42]

In addition to these community mapping activities, youths also worked on self-selected community research and engagement projects on neighborhood issues. Covello writes:

> Each student was required to select a problem and follow it through. The group studying the problems of the slums was expected to make a personal investigation of actual slum conditions. The group studying the problems of the 'melting pot' had to ascertain through actual observation and personal investigation the difficulties presented in the adjustment of racial differences and animosity.[43]

The results of these community projects were presented to the wider public, sometimes in the form of community photography. Covello writes about the interdependence of community problem solving and how one of his students noted this connection in a series of interracial photographs he took. Of the final photo, entitled "the forgotten man—the refuse of the depression," the boy wrote: "His problems are our problems, because if we do not help him solve his, ours will never be solved."[44]

Flint Community Schools

The practice of community schools continued to develop and expand with the vision of "the community becoming the school." One of the most extension experiments was undertaken by the Charles Stewart Mott Foundation in Flint, Michigan, where Frank J. Manley launched the Community School Program in 1936. Throughout that school year, fifteen school buildings provided planned community activities. The organizers, however, found this school-based approach flawed because of the lack of community ownership.

To address this concern, the Mott Foundation hired six staff members to do home visits in the local community to build neighborhood interest and learn more about the community. After an intensive six-week community building training course, the staff members surveyed people in the neighborhood, discovering the conditions of people from the perspectives of where they lived. As a result of these visits, a cooperative planning process was developed with teachers, parents, and social service agencies involved as partners in the planning of activities.

The Flint program continued to expand and evolve. In 1951, the Freeman Community School was built and all the planning was done in partnership with the community—from design and construction, to programs and activities. By 1959, nearly every school had a community school administrator and it became a national model known as "the city of lighted schoolhouses."[45]

Contemporary Community Schools

"Good schools depend on strong communities, and strong communities require good schools. This is the logic driving renewed interest in a time-honored education approach: community schools," writes Martin Blank, director of the Coalition for Community Schools, an alliance of more than 160 national, state, and local educational, youth development, family support, and community development organizations.[46] In the Coalition for Community Schools' report on community schools, *Making the Difference: Research and Practice in Community Schools*, a review of the research found that community schools provide:

- Significant and widespread gains in academic achievement and in essential areas of nonacademic development,
- Increased family stability and greater family involvement with schools,
- Increased teacher satisfaction and more positive school environments,
- Better use of school buildings and increased security and pride in neighborhoods.[47]

While the community schools of the great Flint experiment waned with funding cuts, the essential ideas have been reborn in schools throughout the country. The present examples of community schools have at least three variations. First, in an approach that might be termed the "building community in schools" model, schools attempt to build community inside the school building with the people most directly connected to student learning, including students, teachers, administrators, and parents. The second approach, the "settlement in a school" model, invites local community organizations to participate in learning and advocacy work inside the school building. The final approach for community schools, the "many lighted schoolhouses" model, uses the school building as the primary, but not sole location for academic and community development.

The ideas for the first approach—building community inside schools—has been championed by an impressive group of educators through the Coalition of Essential Schools and are described, for example, by Thomas Sergiovanni's *Building Community in Schools*, Deborah Meier's *The Power of Their Ideas*, and others in the small schools movement.[48] Sergiovanni's research typifies this approach in his emphasis on advocating for schools to act as communities rather than organizations. When this occurs, he argues, community building is embodied in the school's policy structure and community values are at the center of the school.

Deborah Meier's leadership as principal for more than twenty years at Central Park East and now at Mission Hill in Boston provides compelling examples of community building inside schools. In *The Power of Their Ideas*, Meier describes her success at creating a community school in a Harlem neighborhood in Harlem where more than 90 percent of the students graduate and most go on to attend college. Meier illustrates the possibility for starting small, successful public schools that foster a democratic community and inspire children to learn.

The second approach builds community through connections with local neighborhoods and community organizations with the school acting as the social center. For example, beginning in 1992, the Children's Aid Society and the New York City Public Schools have partnered to initiative community schools with this approach. Sometimes termed "the settlement in a school" model, these community schools combine learning with health, mental health, social service, and recreational services in schools located in low-income neighborhoods in New York City.[49] The Children's Aid Society currently has thirteen community school partnerships in three New York City neighborhoods, offering a full range of supports and professional services to children and families, including health, welfare, dental, and social services in the school building itself, as well as extended day, summer, and lifelong learning opportunities.

The Children's Aid Society offers a school-based version of the settlement house tradition with community institutions brought into the school building as partners. This brings a host of community professionals into a centralized location to care for young people's growth. "In these schools, a teacher can walk down the hall to tell a social worker about a student whose grades have suddenly dropped, and a counselor can stop by a classroom to see if a student is showing any signs of improvement," writes the Children's Aid Society in describing the services and resources they provide in *Building a Community School.* The guide continues, "The community school means that, for children, teachers, and parents alike, help is just a step away."[50] The Children's Aid Society creates a tremendous structure for comprehensive education, especially the fluid way the extended day connects with the classroom and school-day activities.

The final community school approach, unlike the Meier and Sergiovanni case examples or that of the Children's Aid Society, makes a deliberate attempt to build educative communities outside as well as inside schools. New York City undertook a bold experiment with the Beacon Schools in 1991, which takes their name directly from the old "lighted schoolhouse" community school idea. The Beacon Schools are funded and directed by the Department of Youth and Community Development (formerly the Department of Youth Services), rather than the Board of Education, freeing them from the school bureaucracy that often stifles innovation. The Beacon Schools, considered a "success story" by leaders in community youth development, such as Karen Pittman, and researchers, such as Lisbeth Schorr, have grown rapidly. These school and community-based centers now operate throughout New York City, with eighty centers in 2007, up from ten centers in 1991.[51]

The purpose of these "many lighted schoolhouses" is to allow community-based organizations to utilize school buildings during nonschool hours for youth activities and community enhancement. Beacons are open after school, evenings, and on weekends, as well as during the summer and school vacations, an average of ten to twelve hours per day. The activities of each Beacon are left for the neighborhood to decide: the only requirements are that activities are community-based, safe, and constructive, and that they include a community advisory council. Beacons are encouraged to partner with as many community organizations as possible, offering community-building activities to young people and families, such as community service projects, GED classes, neighborhood safety ventures, sports tournaments, family nights, and youth planning councils. Beacons work with block associations on neighborhood safety and with community merchant associations to assess community needs; they also initiate voting registration drives, park cleanups, and immunizations drives.[52]

Each of these three contemporary models of community schools offers important models of community schools. The first illustrates the importance of building close, trusting relationships for learning. The Children's Aid Society offers an important model of school-centered community schools. Finally, the Beacons give us a more pronounced community-based application of community schools. Together, they embody current applications of Dewey's vision of the community playing a major role in educational development of youth and the community itself.

Engaged Colleges and Universities

John Dewey's initial vision of the school as a social center did not directly address colleges and universities as institutions for community or democratic improvement. In fact, while Dewey was involved in a great deal of public and community work over the course of his life, he never articulates a vision for the university as a social center. Perhaps not surprisingly given the limited access to higher education at the time, he also never called on colleges and universities to play a significant role in the creation of schools as social centers.[53] However, the schools as a social center, settlement house, and community school movement stand as models for colleges and universities, as illustrated by former U.S. Commissioner of Education Ernest Boyer's call for a larger public purpose in higher education.

The vision set forth by Boyer's October 1995 speech is reminiscent of John Dewey's address for schools to be social centers. In this latest conception, Boyer, who was also the president of the Carnegie Foundation for the Advancement of Teaching, asks that universities act not as social centers, but as "schools of engagement." Boyer called on colleges and universities to practice a larger public purpose when he wrote:

> At one level, the scholarship of engagement means connecting the rich resources of the university to our most pressing social, civic, and ethical problems. . . . Campuses would be viewed by both students and professors not as isolated islands, but as staging grounds for action.
>
> At a deeper level I have this growing conviction that what is also needed is not just more programs, but a larger purpose, a larger sense of mission, a larger clarity of direction in the nation's life as we move toward century twenty-one.[54]

In Service to Democracy

Boyer's vision recalls the ideals of the early mission of land grant universities, which were created to serve the nation. Beginning with the federal Morrill Act in 1862, institutions of higher education were charged with connecting their missions with the broader public. This act gave federal land to each state for the creation of public land grant universities. The Hatch Act of 1887 and the Smith-Lever Act of 1914 formally cemented these efforts by creating the cooperative extension system in land grant institutions to bring university knowledge to farmers in rural communities.[55]

Thus, service to democracy has historically played an important function for higher education. William Rainer Harper, the first president of the University of Chicago, placed higher education as a central agency for creating a democratic society. In 1902, with Dewey as a faculty member on his campus, Harper gave a speech that called on universities to play a significant role in local communities and the broader democracy. Democratic engagement, he proposed, would not only transform the community, but also the university. Harper said:

> A university which will adapt itself to urban influence, which will undertake to serve as an expression of urban civilization, and which is compelled to meet the demands of an urban environment, will in the end become something essentially different from a university located in a village or small city. Such an institution will in time differentiate itself from other institutions. It will gradually take on new characteristics both outward and inward, and it will ultimately form a new type of university.[56]

Harper was not alone in making calls for a "new type of university." In 1908, Charles Eliot, then president of Harvard University, summarized a vision of higher education in service to democracy:

> At bottom most of the American institutions of higher education are filled with the modern democratic spirit of serviceableness. Teachers and students alike are profoundly moved by the desire to serve the democratic community. . . . All the colleges boast of the serviceable men they have trained, and regard the serviceable patriot as their ideal product. This is a thoroughly democratic conception of their function.[57]

The spirit of the university engaged with communities and in service to democracy, as described by Boyer, Harper, Eliot, and many others, developed throughout the twentieth century. One example is the innovative work of Liberty Hyde Bailey, the dean of the New York State College of Agriculture at Cornell University, who helped make Cornell a "people's college" in the early twentieth century. Another important model is "the Wisconsin idea" that offered "to teach anybody-anything-anywhere" in its efforts to actualize a commitment to public service. In addition, colleges and universities played an important role in the recovery from the Great Depression, research during World War II, international development work through the Peace Corps, and work within the nation's schools. And since the GI Bill in 1944 and the development of community colleges, higher education is more involved in providing civic skills, values, and knowledge to a larger percentage of the American population.[58]

Challenges to a Civic Mission

And yet, even as access to higher education has increased, many colleges and universities have become more detached from their public missions. The dominant culture within higher education has helped fuel a rise in specialized, professional practice that deemphasizes the importance of the contributions made to community and civic life. With the growth of specialized fields of knowledge, the link between learning and social purpose has become increasingly separated. Moreover, a consumer-driven model with marketplace values is overtaking the university, seen in unfettered distance learning and, most dramatically, with the rapid rise of the University of Phoenix and other for-profit universities with no campus, organized student body, or permanent faculty.

In addition, reward structures for faculty are based on research and publication in obscure scholarly journals, not on quality teaching—never mind commitment to public work. At the same time, public-spirited faculty often feel powerless to change the structures that stifle them. In a series of interviews with faculty at the University of Minnesota, for instance, Harry Boyte found that the university's institutional culture and communal sense had become balkanized and marketplace values were overwhelming all other values. The detachment of higher education and a weakening concern for public responsibility can perhaps best be seen by looking at the neighborhoods filled with urban decay where so many of the world's "best universities" are located.[59] It can also be noted in the decrease in public confidence in higher education, evidenced by the severe cuts to public funding of higher education by elected state legislatures around the country.

In *Beyond the Campus*, David Maurrasse raises some of the issues making it difficult for campuses to make long-term and genuine commitments to community partnerships:

> Being helpful . . . is to hold the needs of the communities as high as those of the institutions or individual faculty, students, or administrators involved. It is to be patient and build trusting relationships. It is to be around for the long haul. This all goes back to the institution's commitment. A course lasts three or four months. Students are on campus for a few years. Faculty research projects last for a few years. Foundation grants always come to an end. Communities, however, are permanent.[60]

Given all these obstacles to engagement, Maurrasse concludes by asking, "How can higher education ensure that its commitment is genuine?"

Toward a Civic Mission

Although the challenges of privatization, specialization, and fragmentation are daunting, many colleges and universities are making genuine institutional commitments to civic engagement. In the *Chronicle of Higher Education,* Ernest Boyer calls on colleges and universities to overcome these challenges in an effort to create a "new American college." Describing the crisis in impoverished schools and neighborhoods, Boyer tellingly asks, "Do colleges really believe they can ignore the social pathologies that surround schools and erode the educational foundations of our nations?"[61] In a new American college, university professors, staff, and students apply their knowledge and skills to real-life problems, use the experience to revise their theories, and become what Donald Schön termed "reflective practitioners."[62]

In some significant ways higher education is attempting to heed Boyer's calls with an increasingly robust civic renewal movement, starting with the creation of Campus Outreach Opportunity League (COOL) and Campus Compact in the mid-1980s to promote civic engagement among colleges and universities. These efforts began primarily around community service and expanded in the 1990s with attempts to institutionalize community service into the academic curriculum with what has been termed "service-learning." Today, undergraduates around the country are involved in this pursuit.

The institutional impact is dramatic. Over the course of the 1990s came the founding of the Corporation for National and Community Service as well as the Community Outreach Partnership Center (COPC) program from the Department of Housing and Urban Development—government programs to support university involvement in communities. In addition, Campus Compact has grown from a few hundred members to more than 1,000 institutions with affiliated state compacts in thirty-one states, and COOL recently held its twentieth annual student conference on community involvement for thousands of college students. The attempt to concentrate on the academic side of the university—arguably the most important, but difficult venue for change—has seen success as well. For example, service-learning now has the *Michigan Journal of Community Service Learning,* a national service-learning journal; and Campus Compact has worked to institutionalize civic engagement through trainings for academic departments and partnerships with disciplinary associations.

Even the Princeton Review and *U.S. News and World Report* are noticing the importance of civic engagement and service-learning. In 2005, Campus Compact and the Princeton Review published *Colleges with a Con-*

science, the first-of-its kind guide for high school students to use civic engagement as criteria for their selection process;[63] *U.S. News and World Report* includes a listing of the nation's top service-learning colleges. And leading institutions of higher education make major commitments to civic engagement, notably, the University of Pennsylvania, Portland State University, Tufts University, Miami Dade College, the University of Minnesota, the University of Utah, Georgetown University, and DePaul University, representing different types of college and universities. As a result, it is now common for colleges and universities to have a center that promotes service-learning and civic engagement. For instance, today 83 percent of Campus Compact member schools house a Community Service or Service-Learning Office, up from only 50 percent in 1995.

The University of Pennsylvania, led by Ira Harkavy's Center for Community Partnerships, is the institution of higher education perhaps most noted for its commitment to collaborating with schools and communities for educational improvement. The Center for Community Partnerships, founded in 1992, began with the notion that the resources of the university could be creatively utilized to address the problems of urban America. Through this center, the University of Pennsylvania sponsors a series of community schools, arts and health programs in the West Philadelphia neighborhood, action research seminars, and many other community partnerships.

Based on almost twenty years of working with local schools and communities, Harkavy and Benson reflect on the importance of an ecology of civic learning when they write,

> It became clear that educational change could not be accomplished by focusing only on schools and schooling. We increasingly realized . . . that school and school system change are intrinsically connected to community change and community mobilization and that effective community change depends on reforming the local public schools into 'good' public schools.[64]

Building on the influences of John Dewey and Jane Addams, as well as the community school movement, their efforts indicate the overlapping connections between the various elements within education in the community. The successful creation and operation of the Sayre Health Promotion and Disease Prevention Center, for example, work to improve community health through democratically identifying and democratically trying to solve a highly complex, highly significant, real-world, local community problem that, by its very nature, requires sustained inter-school and interdisciplinary collaboration.[65]

The efforts of engaged colleges and universities have rippled nationally. For example, Campus Compact has been promoting civic engagement of students, faculty, administrators, and staff with the goal of creating "engaged campuses"—colleges and universities utilizing all the resources at their disposal toward democratic revitalization. In this pursuit, Campus Compact issued a declaration signed by more than 500 college presidents from around the country describing the civic role for institutions of higher education. *The Presidents' Declaration on the Civic Responsibility of Higher Education* calls for a "recommitment of higher education to its civic purposes."[66]

Students have also played a leadership role in demanding that higher education take serious its public mission to educate for civic, as well as workforce, preparation. Few documents speak more clearly to this demand than the *Oklahoma Students' Civic Resolution*, a public statement issued by student leaders from more than a dozen colleges and universities across Oklahoma:

> We declare that it is our responsibility to become an engaged generation with the support of our political leaders, education institutions, and society. . . . The mission of our state higher education institutions should be to educate future citizens about their civic as well as professional duties. We urge our institutions to prioritize and implement civic education in the classroom, in research, and in service to the community.[67]

Today, Dewey's call for all schools to act as social centers speaks directly to institutions of higher education—and is especially relevant now as the rates of people attending institutions of higher education increase.[68] The vision of educational institutions standing as social centers connected with communities over the long haul is an essential part of the politics of civic education reform in higher education. The examples cited earlier indicate that the obstacles for colleges and universities participating in civic engagement can certainly be overcome.

Colleges and universities have become perhaps the most important single institution in this pursuit because of their unique ability to both leverage community engagement and educate future civic professionals. Put simply, colleges and universities can both engage with local communities and also prepare a new generation of democratic community practitioners. Colleges and universities have also played an important role in each of the following cases.

Hull House, Highlander, and the Neighborhood Learning Community: Why These Cases?

This partial review of the history of a different type of education illustrates a powerful tradition that reaches beyond the schools to educate for democracy. It seems that the United States has a rich history that calls for utilizing the ecology of civic learning.

In the next three chapters, I examine three of the most powerful historical and contemporary cases in greater detail. In the unique and diverse cases of Hull House, Highlander Folk School, and the Neighborhood Learning Community, I offer detailed examples of why community matters for civic learning.

Hull House provides a citizen-centered model in which people of diverse class and ethnic backgrounds live and work side-by-side in an urban neighborhood. The issues they addressed, especially on the role of immigrant contributions and cultural identity in American democracy, are vital in the contemporary struggles in communities throughout the United States. Hull House developed important practices and models—such as the Labor Museum—for addressing these problems. Hull House also illustrates an approach that enabled young activists to lead a life committed to eliminating injustice as co-educators with the poor. This was done with a solid foundation: Jane Addams's unbending belief in democracy and the power of ordinary people to shape our world.

This same belief is at the foundation for the ideas of Myles Horton and the democratic educational practices of the Highlander Folk School, though in a very different setting. Highlander used workshop retreats to bring people together outside their home communities to reflect and plan for collaborative action back home. Reading about Highlander in the simple, straightforward language of Myles Horton has inspired many civic educators. Horton is an educational guide for those interested in respecting the experiences of all learners and making community a central democratic value.

Although there are many promising approaches, such as service-learning and extracurricular activities, for schools to extend into communities to promote civic education, my interest in the Neighborhood Learning Community on the West Side of St. Paul, Minnesota, stems from the ecological nature of its approach: it attempts to use the whole community in connecting education with civic life. With the Neighborhood Learning Community, the community also reaches into the local schools and institutions of higher education for resources to complement their community-led efforts to create a culture of civic learning.

In addition, the Neighborhood Learning Community deliberately draws on the lessons of both Hull House and the Highlander Folk School in its work. These historical traditions are put in a contemporary context where learning in everyday life is the basis for community building, school improvement, and democratic revitalization.

While my focus is on three diverse models where community is playing a role in linking learning with civic engagement, many other significant programs and models could have been explored (some of these, such as the social center movement in the early twentieth century and the campus–school–community partnerships at the University of Pennsylvania, were discussed previously). I chose these three models because of the uniqueness and diversity of approaches they represent for addressing essential issues of their times and places.

In the early twentieth century, the issues were immigration, urbanization, and industrialization. In the mid-twentieth century, the issue was civil rights. In the early twenty-first century, the issues include increasing consumerism, fragmentation, and professionalization; declining political and civic involvement; widening inequality; and deteriorating inner-city neighborhoods and schools. Each case, however, in its own context, uses education writ large within an asset-based, citizen-centered approach to confront the problems of its time. And each case provides important lessons about the importance of community in educating for democracy.

Chapter Three

Hull House

In these days of criticism of democracy as a political institution, Miss Addams has reminded us that democracy is not a form but a way of living together and working together. I doubt if any other one agency can be found which has touched so many people and brought to them a conception of the real meaning of the spirit of the common life.

—John Dewey, 1930, on the fortieth anniversary of Hull House

In this first case study, I examine the educational approach of Chicago's original settlement house, Hull House, beginning with the ideas of its charismatic founder, Jane Addams. An examination of Hull House sets a solid foundation for why community matters, as it is perhaps the most extensive early attempt at comprehensive, relational, and public education that nurtures the ecology of civic learning. It is therefore essential to examine this case for lessons that may be illuminated for contemporary efforts to educate for democracy. In this pursuit, I have come to agree with historian Ellen Lagemann, who concludes that Addams "offers important grist for rethinking what education can and cannot do."[1]

An Educator for Democracy

Two years after Dewey's "School as a Social Centre" speech, Jane Addams hinted at a more fundamental shift in educational practice than Dewey's conception of schools as central to community life. Addams called for *communities* to be the center of education. Addams asked her readers to imagine what public schools would look like if they followed the educational practices of Hull House, the social settlement that Addams had formed with Ellen Gates Starr fifteen years before. "We could imagine the business man teaching the immigrant his much needed English and arithmetic," she wrote, "and receiving in return lessons in the handling of tools and materials so that they should assume in his mind a totally different significance from that [which] the factory gives them." In the same place, Addams argued, one might see immigrant Italian women learning English in the kitchen while they teach their instructors "how to cook the delicious macaroni, such a different thing from the semi-elastic product which Americans honor with that name."[2]

This was not a new concept for Addams. In fact, she had been articulating this conception of education and schooling since the founding of Hull House. This description, however, offers one of the earliest descriptions of "education in the community." It is what Addams meant when she termed the social settlements movement a "protest against a restricted view of education."[3]

Hull House's approach, then, made the community, in the words of Jane Addams, "a center for social and educational activity."[4] She envisioned Hull House as a force for education that connected the many places where people learn in a neighborhood. "Its force was centrifugal," writes Lawrence Cremin. "Instead of drawing educational functions into itself, it reached out into the community to help organize social relations in such a way that community itself would become educative."[5]

In the process of reaching into the neighborhood, Addams became aware of the power of community learning. "Because Jane Addams remained aloof from most 'professional' thinking about education she understood that an infinite variety of experiences, associated with an infinite variety of institutions and sometimes not associated with any institution, can shape, expand, elaborate, refine, and otherwise change the ways in which people perceive themselves and their surroundings," Ellen Lagemann observes. She continues that this nonprofessional approach enabled the settlement "to act in relation to those perceptions and . . . associate for purposes of thought and action with other people."[6] An approach that realized the value of nonprofessionals and the multitude of places that people learn also helped Addams recognize that the educative functions of Hull House could not be done in isolation; it required a whole community.

Soon after founding Hull House, Addams realized that education was also inexplicably linked with civic life. Thus, Hull House increasingly tied its educational efforts with attempts to bring about political reform. During the Progressive Era, Jane Addams was an articulate voice on nearly every reform issue and her settlement house was a practical response to many of these issues.[7] Hull House addressed political issues as varied as the corruption of elected politicians, child labor, labor organizing, arts education, war and peace, treatment of new Americans, and the need for sanitary streets. In taking on these issues, Jane Addams was a founder of social work; a champion for children's rights, immigrants' contributions, and international peace; and a powerful woman in times when there were limited opportunities for women in public life. More important, for the purposes of this exploration, Jane Addams was an educator for democracy.

Overview

There is no shortage of writing about Hull House, including Jane Addams's dozen books and hundreds of published articles and speeches. Most famous among these is Addams's autobiographical *Twenty Years at Hull House* in which she reflects on her life as embodied in the early years at Hull House.[8] More recently, University of Chicago political philosopher Jean Bethke Elshtain published a biography (one of several in the past few years) along with an edited collection of Addams's writings, *The Jane Addams Reader*, as historians Christopher Lasch and Ellen Lagemann had done in previous decades.[9]

Jane Addams, in fact, is undergoing something of a revival. Her alma mater, Rockford College, uses Addams as the centerpiece of its marketing materials to attract civic-minded students. And three of Addams's books, *The Spirit of Youth and the City Streets*, *Democracy and Social Ethics*, and *The Long Road of Woman's Memory* were recently republished, indicating the increased interest in making her ideas available.[10]

In all of these writings and public recognitions, one will quickly find no shortage of praise for Jane Addams and her heroic life, nor a shortage of critics. Yet even with this renewed interest, the writings of Addams and the history of Hull House are little known beyond the field of social work. Addams is largely ignored by feminist theory, philosophy, and sociology. Moreover, even though she was an educational theorist and practitioner who also had a profound influence on the thinking of John Dewey, she is barely mentioned in the history of education. With some exceptions, more practical fields, such as service-learning and civic education, are also relatively silent on the contributions of Jane Addams and Hull House.[11]

This is a significant oversight. These settlement workers' pioneering efforts to live and work in the West Side neighborhood of Chicago provide a pragmatic example of one of the great social experiments with democracy in action. These women were not utopian idealists looking to escape the realities of society. Rather, they moved into the center of a low-income, urban community and lived as neighbors, friends, and fellow citizens.

These experiments provide important lessons for how we educate for democracy today. Addams allows us a glimpse into the origins of service-learning as practice, not theory. A history of service-learning that takes account of Addams also locates the origins of service-learning not in the schools, but in the community. And it places the origins of service-learning squarely in the movement for the expansion of the role of women in public life. Jane Addams's work is also a valuable reminder that service-learning may be understood not only as an educational technique, but also as a craft, whose greatest value is the unpredictable creativity that it brings to our public life. Each of these lessons for service-learning—practice, community, gender, and craft—is also vital to our contemporary efforts in civic education.[12]

The practical, community-based, feminist, craft-like approach exhibited by Hull House residents was evident in the holistic experiences used at the settlement. It connected neighborhood residents of all ages with opportunities for learning in a diverse set of community institutions. In *The Second Twenty Years at Hull House,* Addams reflects on her then forty years at Hull House with the awareness of the multitude of approaches necessary to alleviate social problems. Addams writes:

> The settlements have often been accused of scattering their forces; as institutions they are both philanthropic and educational; in their approach to social problems they call now upon the sociologist, now upon the psychiatrist; they seek the services of artists, economists, gymnasts, case-workers, dramatists, trained nurses; one day they beg the anthropologist for a clue to a new immigration, the next they boast that one of their pupils is playing in the symphony orchestra.[13]

Addams wisely concludes, "In response to the irrefutable charge of weakness in multiform activity, we are accustomed to reply that even so we are not as varied and complex as life itself."[14]

The settlements multiform—and ecological—response to social problems at the turn of the twentieth century took place at the local level. College-educated women lived and worked as neighbors with poor immigrants. The residents of Hull House connected the stories, lives, and issues they saw day-to-day with large public ideas and co-created practical solutions. They responded to children not wanting candy because of excessive time working in candy factories, for instance, by advocating for legislation to outlaw child labor; and to garbage in the streets by becoming inspectors and systematically studying the neighborhood. Hull House residents responded to the neighborhood with a reciprocal, intergenerational approach that valued the knowledge and talents of ordinary people. They provided classes, lectures, athletics, and clubs. Hull House was a neighborhood community center, one of the first, but its residents made the nation the audience for the issues they encountered.[15]

Hull House went on to become the most famous settlement house of its time with Addams as a national spokesperson for the movement. Settlements gave women from upper-class backgrounds the opportunity to make significant public contributions. They also addressed the seminal issues at the turn of the last century: rapid industrialization, urbanization, and a large increase of non–English-speaking immigrants from Europe. Connecting these forces allowed the settlement idea to spread rapidly. In 1891, two years after the founding of Hull House, there were six settlements in the United States; by 1897 there were seventy-four. It quickly jumped to 100 in 1900, doubled to 200 in 1905 and then doubled again, so that by 1910 there were more than 400 settlements.[16]

Hull House was a "spearhead for reform" in this national movement and its efforts led to many significant reforms. In its first year, Hull House opened a kindergarten; it established the first public playground in Chicago as well as the first citizenship preparation classes in the United States. Hull House had a music school, drama and choral groups, a nursery, and day-care center. It had a Shakespeare Club, Plato Club, and university extension classes (taught by people from the university). It offered summer camps and courses on cooking, along with clubs for boys, girls, and women. In 1900, Hull House created the Labor Museum, a school for immigrant adults to teach the crafts of their homelands, which is described in detail below.[17]

Hull House was termed a "salon of democracy" by a visiting writer because of the way it served as a meeting place for conversations by such a diverse group of people. The observer reported, "There passes a procession of Greek fruit vendors, university professors, mayors, alderman, clubwomen, factory inspectors, novelists, reporters, policemen, Italian washwomen, socialists looking hungrily for all persons yet unconverted, big businessmen finding the solution of the industrial problem in small parts, English members of Parliament, German scientists, and all other sorts and conditions of men from the river wards of the city of Chicago and from the far corners of the five continents."[18] Addams concludes from these experiences that ordinary people were interested in big ideas and great things, told in a simple, practical, and straightforward manner.[19]

Hull House also did advocacy work, fighting for the elimination of sweatshops, sanitary streets, child labor laws, juvenile courts, and international peace. Hull House even got involved in local politics, trying for two terms to unseat the corrupt Chicago alderman in the 19th ward—with little success. It was in these elections that Addams saw the virtues of neighborhood politics; in fact, Addams often claimed that the methods of the corrupt ward boss were more democratic than those of detached reformers. Unlike the reformers, the corrupt politicians were "engaged in the great moral effort of getting the mass to express itself, and of adding this mass energy and wisdom to the community as a whole."[20] Finally, Hull House did engaged research, including the publication of *Hull House Maps and Papers*, the first sociological investigation of a neighborhood.[21]

Lawrence Cremin found that the common theme in all these activities was mutual education: reciprocal learning between neighborhood residents and Hull House settlement workers. These practices, he contends, then "became one of the prime sources of reformist educational theory during the Progressive Era."[22] It has also impacted reformist educational practices during the civil rights movement, as seen with Highlander Folk School and educational networks today, such as the Neighborhood Learning Community in St. Paul, Minnesota. Mutual and reciprocal education is central to each of these efforts to create educative communities, as seen in the following chapters.

The emphasis on mutual education was evident in much of Hull House's programming—which grew rapidly. When Addams and Starr founded Hull House, they occupied the second floor of the original house on Halsted Street and used an additional room on the first floor. Hull House soon became the equivalent of a modern-day college campus with multiple buildings for residency, programming, and entertainment. By 1891, the settlement offered more than fifty clubs and classes utilized by more than a thousand people every week. Each weekday, every room in the house was filled with people. In the early 1890s, Hull House expanded to another building, adding an art gallery. By the turn of the century, it added a coffee house and gymnasium; a Children's House with rooms for a kindergarten, nursery, and music school; an additional building for the Jane Club, a cooperative residency for working girls; and a new coffeehouse and theater. There was constant construction, and by 1907 the single floor—and more powerfully, the idea of mutual education for democracy—had expanded to thirteen buildings sprawling over a large city block, as it would remain until 1963.[23]

Overcoming the "Snare of Preparation"

Jane Addams was born in 1860, the year that Abraham Lincoln became president, on the eve of the Civil War and the forthcoming social, political, and intellectual changes the war would bring. Prior to founding Hull House, Jane Addams spent several years searching for her way to contribute to the world. There were not many options for women in public life at the end of the ninteenth century. Still not afforded the right to vote, even college-educated women were pressured to marry and take one of the few appropriate career options, such as teaching or nursing.

In the period following her graduation from Rockford Seminary, Addams struggled with depression and chronic illnesses. She started and then dropped out of medical school. She traveled to Europe several times searching for a larger purpose. Looking back in her autobiography, Addams terms this period, aptly, "the snare of preparation." Addams writes:

> It was not until years afterward that I came upon Tolstoy's phrase "the snare of preparation," which he insists we spread before the feet of young people, hopelessly entangling them in a curious inactivity at the very period of life when they are longing to construct the world anew and to conform it to their own ideals.[24]

Addams's period of preparation, however, lasted much shorter than most. During her travels, Addams found a promising model with young people overcoming their inactivity by working across the class divide in England. In 1888, she visited the first settlement house, Toynbee Hall in London. Samuel Barnett and his wife, Henrietta Rowland, started Toynbee Hall in 1884 to bring the benefits of college life (along with Christian ideals) to the poor by inviting university students to live among the poor and respond to the problems of an urban neighborhood. The settlement house, as one historian noted, "was meant to be a civic community, based upon a common denominator of citizenship in the largest sense of the word. . . . It was an experiment in democracy—which was no mean feat at that time and place."[25]

Addams received a tour of the settlement, interviewed its residents, and came away impressed. Addams decided that on her return to the United States—at quite a young age, twenty-nine—she would start a social settlement house with women residents in a poor neighborhood in Chicago. She recruited her friend Ellen Gates Starr to join her.

Together, Addams and Starr founded Hull House on September 18, 1889. Addams wrote of this substantial undertaking: "I had confidence that although life itself might contain many difficulties, the period of mere passive receptivity had come to an end, and I had at last finished with the everlasting 'preparation for life,' however ill-prepared I might be."[26] She would have no way of knowing at that time that their decision would have a substantial impact on an entire era of reform efforts, many of which continue to this day.

At 335 Halsted Street (in 1909 due to zoning changes, the same address became the famed 800 South Halsted St.) in Chicago's 19th ward,

Addams and Starr began with a modest plan to live as neighbors with poor immigrants. Hull House, however, was filled with an ambitious democratic vision. It was hoping to provide cultural transformation in urban America, implicit in Addams's idea that the settlement "was an attempt to express the meaning of life in terms of life itself."[27] This experiment was not simply meant to help poor immigrants. Like service-learning today the settlements hoped to address pressing "objective" needs in the community, but also provide a creative, educational "subjective" outlet for college-educated people by putting their idealism into action.

Giving idealism concrete opportunities for application was a core ingredient for success. In an address in 1892, Addams gives us an insight into a core dilemma that still demoralizes young people (as well as those older)—the feeling of powerlessness. Addams writes:

> We have in America a fast-growing number of cultivated young people who have no recognized outlet for their active faculties. They hear constantly of the great social maladjustment, but no way is provided for them to change it, and their uselessness hangs upon them heavily. . . . [T]he sense of uselessness is the severest shock which the human system can sustain, and that if persistently sustained, it results in atrophy of function. These young people have had advantages of college, European travel, and of economic study, but they are sustaining this shock.[28]

Addams and Starr jumped in to tackle life and overcome the atrophy that comes from inactivity and powerlessness. In this, they were certainly in over their heads, as Addams acknowledged. But that was the plan. "Of course we are undertaking more than we ourselves can do, that is part of the idea," Addams writes to her sister during the early months on Halsted Street.[29]

One afternoon in the early days of the settlement, a young woman rushed into Hull House and announced that an unwed girl in a tenement down the street was having a baby all by herself. She could not afford a doctor, her mother was at work, and neighbors refused to help because she was unmarried. Addams and her settlement colleague Julia Lanthrop responded and delivered the baby.[30] In her last book, Addams beautifully captures the scene of the neighborhood just before dinner time. While they had doubts and thought they might be in over their heads, these early settlement pioneers also felt an assuredness that they were on the right path. Addams writes:

> I vividly recall through the distance of forty-five years after that as we walked back from the tenement house stirred as we were by the mystery

of birth, and seeing the neighborhood at its most attractive moment when the fathers were coming back from work, the children playing near the doorstep to be ready for supper which the mother was cooking inside, I explained: "This doing things that we don't know how to do is going too far. Why did we let ourselves be rushed into midwifery?" To which [Lanthrop] replied: "If we have to begin to hew down to the line of our ignorance, for goodness' sake don't let us begin at the humanitarian end. To refuse to respond to a poor girl in the throes of childbirth would be a disgrace to us forevermore. If Hull House does not have its roots in human kindness, it is no good at all."[31]

We can only imagine how many times early settlement workers were called on to do things in fields far beyond their expertise. These experiences most certainly stretched these community practitioners, not as professionals, but as citizens. Addams's writing is filled with stories of responding with improvisational, spontaneous care as an engaged, concerned neighbor—especially in the early days of Hull House. One story recalls Addams being called to a fire in the neighborhood to give "permission" to slaughter horses that had been injured. Another discusses the mediating role played by Hull House in a dispute between the police and the neighborhood after three Italian boys were shot by a police officer. This is a role played today by judges, lawyers, teachers, social workers, and other professionals. Hull House residents assumed these roles as neighbors and citizens.[32]

Beyond Cultural Uplift

Hull House did not exactly start with the idea of acting as equal partners with its neighbors. The most damning critique of Hull House is the perception that Addams and the residents of Hull House were working not just for democracy and social justice, but also for social control—attempting to bring high culture to the low-income immigrants of Chicago. Early attempts at "cultural uplift" included, among other things, an art exhibit wherein Hull House hung reproductions of paintings by great European artists throughout the settlement. This idea, which was conceived by Addams and Starr prior to moving into Hull House, also included a lending program allowing families to borrow art for display in their tenements.

Addams originally appreciated that the lending program brought some beauty to run-down homes. "A few doors down the street a tiny bedroom has been changed from a place in which a fragile factory girl slept the sleep of the exhausted into one where she 'just loves to lie in bed and

look at my pictures; it's so like art class,'" Addams bragged.[33] Upon reflection, though, Addams and Starr decided that uplift alone was not sufficient based on several assumptions they had made, which proved to be
inaccurate when faced with real experiences.

First, uplift ignored the cultural gifts and talents of immigrant communities, immediately evident once the settlement workers spent much
time with their neighbors. Hull House quickly became more collaborative in its programming, bringing in more voices and experiences. Addams tellingly noted in 1895, "All the details were left for the demands of
the neighborhood to determine, and each department has grown from a
discovery made through natural and reciprocal relations."[34]

Second, uplift included false assumptions about the role of settlement workers. By defining them as outside the community, it erected unnecessary barriers between service-providers and recipients. In her
critique of the charitable model and the subsequent class division it reinforced, Addams wrote, "Many of the difficulties in philanthropy come
from an unconscious division of the world into the philanthropists and
those to be helped. It is an assumption of two classes, and against this
class assumption our democratic training revolts as soon as we begin to
act upon it."[35]

Finally, the assumptions within uplift privatized the effort for social
change. As opposed to a private home, Hull House provided public
space that anyone in the community could enjoy, learn from, and collectively act within. For example, a copy of a Rembrandt hanging in one
apartment was for the benefit of only a few people; a public lecture on
Rembrandt could reach hundreds.[36]

Because Hull House residents were there for longer periods of time,
they were able to learn from their early mistakes and inaccurate assumptions. In one of the most pointed examples of learning from its neighbors about how not to respond, Addams recalls how Hull House cared
for an abandoned baby from the neighborhood, providing the best medical treatment available. After they were unable to save the child, the well-
meaning residents of Hull House decided on a county burial. This
decision, however, was seen as inappropriate in the eyes of the neighborhood. When word of this got around, the neighbors took up a collection for the child to be buried "properly." Addams recalls, "It is doubtful
whether Hull House has ever done anything which injured it so deeply in
the minds of some of its neighbors. We were only forgiven by the most in-
dulgent on the ground that we were spinsters and could not know a
mother's heart. No one born and reared in the community could possibly have made a mistake like that. No one who had studied the ethical
standards with any care could have bungled so completely."[37]

Other more mundane mistakes led to action. For instance, on the first Christmas at Hull House—when the new residents knew nothing yet of child labor—children who came to Hull House refused the candy offered to them because they worked all day in a candy factory and could not bear the sight of it. Thus, living in the neighborhood and seeing firsthand the impact of child labor led Hull House residents to advocate on behalf of children's rights, a minimum age for employment, and the elimination of sweatshops.

The early efforts to bring high culture to the poor changed partially out of necessity. Soon after the founding of Hull House, the settlement's residents were thrust into collaborative enterprises that addressed pressing interests, such as garbage removal, health care, and day care. "The residents of Hull House feel increasingly that the educational efforts of a settlement should not be directed to reproduce the college type of culture, but to work out a method and an idea adapted to the immediate situation," Addams wrote.[38] As the residents became increasingly aware of the effect that industrialization and urbanization had on new Americans and their children, Hull House acted accordingly.

Hull House Residents

Prior to its founding, Addams and Starr were concerned about whether Hull House could attract residents to live—or "settle"—among the poor. These fears turned out to be unwarranted. Hull House developed a cooperative living arrangement with many women residents, in addition to some men. Most residents rented rooms and had additional paid work. Residents were also required to go through a probationary period and then stay for at least six months. This unique living and working arrangement attracted some of the most talented, creative, and brave group of women of their generation.

Hull House residents and associates became leaders in fights for justice at the turn of the twentieth century. Aside from co-founder Ellen Gates Starr, fixtures at Hull House who helped shape the programs included Julia Lanthrop, who came to Hull House during its first year and went on to become the first head of the Children's Bureau. Florence Kelley arrived just after Christmas 1891 (a single mother with her three children) and later went on to become Chief Factory Inspector for Illinois and then Secretary of the National Consumers League. Alice Hamilton, a leader in industrial medicine, came to Hull House in 1897 while she was a professor at Women's Medical School of Northwestern University and stayed until 1919 when she became the first woman professor at Harvard Medical School. Early residents such as Mary Smith, Addams's life partner, and then Louise Bowen, Hull House's largest contributor while she was treasurer from 1907 until after Addams's death, provided much-needed financial support again and again for Hull House programs. Even when they left, former residents stayed connected, helped raise funds, and visited often.[39]

Utilizing the resources of the neighborhood to tackle the problems around Halsted Street was a deliberate decision for the early leaders at Hull House, based on reflective practice. After first using Toynbee Hall as a model, the experiences in the actual community enabled the vision of the leaders at Hull House to grow in new and unexpected ways. The influences of Lanthrop, Kelley, Hamilton, and other long-time residents helped catalyze research and political reform; Hull House residents developed reciprocal relations with neighborhood residents to make sustained, long-term commitments to social change.

Hull House residents addressed community issues as co-investigators and colleagues due to the fact that they were also neighbors seeing problems firsthand. "The question is often asked whether all that the House undertakes could not be accomplished without the wear and tear of living on the spot," writes Florence Kelley, who after arriving in the final days of 1891 greatly influenced the shift toward the political and reform-minded work of the settlement. She continues, "The answer is that it could not, grows more assured as time goes on. You must suffer from the dirty streets, the universal ugliness, the lack of oxygen in the air you daily breathe, the endless struggle with soot and dust and insufficient water supply, the hanging from a strap of the overcrowded street car at the end of your day's work; you must send your children to the nearest wretchedly crowded school and see them suffer the consequences, if you are to speak as one having authority and not as the scribes in these matters of the common, daily life and experience." Kelley, who was also a lead author of *Hull House Maps and Papers*, then concludes, "There are many things which you can learn only by way of neighborly contact."[40]

Sustained, neighborly contact gave settlement workers a firsthand view of social problems and inequality in the struggle to build a vibrant democracy. Another long-time resident, Alice Hamilton, who decided to live at Hull House after hearing Addams speak, writes in her autobiography, "In settlement life it is impossible not to see how deep and fundamental are the inequalities in our democratic country."[41]

John Dewey and Jane Addams

The settlement movement focused on reciprocal relations, longer periods of time with people, localized knowledge, and engagement across the lines of race, class, gender, age, and language. It also connected education with democracy. This approach had a lasting impact on a diverse group of theorists, practitioners, and social movements, most notably John Dewey and the school as a social center movement that extended the use of the school building in the early twentieth century, as discussed in chapter two.

John Dewey once remarked that he learned more from people and situations than from books.[42] His relationship with Jane Addams and time spent at Hull House are certainly among the most significant in the philosopher's thinking on education and democracy. This relationship is important for understanding the scope of the influence that Addams had over subsequent educational ideas and practices. For instance, Dewey often used the settlements as a model for public schooling. In a 1915 essay on the school as a social settlement, Dewey concludes, "Closer contact with neighborhood conditions not only enriches school work and strengthens motive force in the pupils, but it increases the service rendered to the community."[43] This belief was born out of his relationship with Addams and Hull House.

Dewey had visited Hull House even before joining the faculty at the University of Chicago. This was early in the existence of Hull House and the young Dewey, then thirty-two years old (Addams was thirty-one), came away impressed. After that visit, Dewey wrote to Addams on January 27, 1892:

> I cannot tell you how much good I got from the stay at Hull House. My indebtedness to you for giving me an insight into matters there is great. While I did not see much of any particular thing I think I got a pretty good idea of the general spirit and method. Every day I stayed there only added to my conviction that you had taken the right way.

Dewey concludes his letter by predicting that other community institutions will apply the experiential educational approaches used by Hull House: "I am confident that 25 years from now the forces now turned in upon themselves in various church and c[ommunity] agencies will be finding outlet very largely through just such channels as you have opened."[44]

This connection to Addams and Hull House grew deeper over many years of friendship. For example, when Dewey's eight-year-old son Gordon died, the memorial service was held at Hull House with Addams officiating; Dewey named his daughter Jane after Miss Addams. Addams's namesake once remarked that her father's "faith in democracy as a guiding force in education took on both sharper and deeper meaning because of Hull House and Jane Addams."[45]

Dewey and Addams saw themselves as part of the same circle. When Dewey moved from Chicago to teach at Columbia in New York City, for instance, he got involved with local settlement houses: Dewey became chairman of the educational committee at Mary Simkhovitch's Greenwich

House, and Lillian Wald from Henry Street Settlement became a colleague.[46] Christopher Lasch, who edited the first major collection of the writings of Addams, notes that "it is difficult to say whether Dewey influenced Jane Addams or Jane Addams influenced Dewey. They influenced each other and generously acknowledged their mutual obligations."[47]

And yet most of the scholarship on their collaborations and mutual influences comes from writings by and about Addams, as opposed to Dewey. Dewey and his subsequent scholars gave much less public recognition to the role Addams (and other women) played on the most famous philosopher of education.[48] Even when Addams is recognized, it is often believed that Dewey is the educational philosopher, while Addams was the educational activist. Cremin disagrees, however, arguing that "it is important to see Jane Addams as a theorist of education in her own right."[49]

It is also worth pointing out that two of Dewey's major works of educational philosophy, "The School as Social Centre" and *Democracy and Education* were heavily influenced by his experience at Hull House, along with his views of citizen involvement in democracy, seen most clearly in *The Public and Its Problems*.[50] One Dewey scholar contends that Dewey's commitment to learning in the community was years ahead of others in the field of education as a result of his relationship with Addams. Through this lens, Dewey was able to analyze "Hull House activities for their broadest educational implications."[51]

Moreover, in his most direct attribution to Hull House as a model for educational practice, "The School as a Social Settlement," Dewey compared the schools with the social settlements and concludes that schools must follow the model of the settlements by also serving the community as widely as possible.[52] The philosopher Charlene Haddock Seigfried tellingly notes that Dewey's ideal community, a "mode of associated living, or conjoint communicated experience," was first made real at Hull House before he put its essence on the page.[53]

The essential distinction between school-centered and community-centered education is paramount in the writings of Addams and Dewey. Both believed in the centrality of learning from experience. Both also believed in the role in education for democratic citizenship. However, Addams shifted the center of education into the community, while Dewey made the school the center of educational activity.[54] Cremin writes:

> But whereas Dewey turned to a reconstructed school and a reconstructed university as levers of social change, Addams assigned what was at best a limited role to schools and universities in the cause of social reform and turned instead to settlements and similar institutions as educational forces that would energize the community to become itself the most potent of all educative forces.[55]

Shifting the Social Center

Hull House vigorously attempted to connect the schools with the families and neighborhoods from which they drew their students. Addams articulated how Hull House made these connections within the context of its comprehensive learning model for children and adults. The same year Dewey was formulating "the school as a social center" concept, Addams articulated a different gravitational center. Addams wrote, "If we admit that in education it is necessary to begin with the experiences which the child already has and to use his spontaneous and social activity, then the city streets begin this education for him in a more natural way than does the school."[56] Hull House provides a concrete example that set the entire community, not just the school, as the center for learning and democratic action.

One of the chief roles played by Hull House is often overlooked, perhaps because of its impressive resume of social intervention and reform work—namely, its role as a mediating institution. Part of that role consisted of offering classes. But an equally important part consisted of acting as a community connector. Hull House connected people in the neighborhood to community institutions, like health centers, as well as formal educational institutions, such as schools, colleges, and universities. Addams often described this work as bringing into the circle of knowledge and fuller life men and women who might otherwise be left outside:

> Perhaps the chief value of a Settlement to its neighborhood, certainly to the newly arrived foreigner, is its office as an information and interpretation bureau. It sometimes seems as if the business of the settlement were that of a commission merchant. Without endowment and without capital itself, it constantly acts between the various institutions of the city and the people for whose benefit these institutions were erected. The hospitals, the country agencies, and State asylums are often but vague rumors to people who need them most. This commission work, as I take it, is of value not only to the recipient, but to the institutions themselves.[57]

The relational "commission work" of the settlement house led residents to connect with local politics, lead reforms in city hall, work with public schools and universities, and connect local immigrants to other much-needed public institutions. Settlement workers became aware of the neighborhood needs, but also became aware of its gifts. Jane Addams claimed that the settlement's unique role in the neighborhood allowed it to see institutions from the perspective of ordinary neighborhood residents; at the same time, because settlement workers were conversant in language of professionals, they provided bridges to larger institutions of power.

Community partnerships within this framework take on greater significance. Addams learned early on that outsiders often made assumptions about Hull House's neighbors, who were referred to as "those
people." While Addams herself might dismiss those assumptions, she pre-
ferred giving "those people" an opportunity to speak for themselves.
Thus, Addams claimed that she never addressed a Chicago audience on
the subject of the settlement and the surrounding community without
inviting a neighbor to go along so that she "might curb any hasty gener-
alization by the consciousness that I had an auditor who knew the conditions more intimately than I could hope to do."[58]

In doing things like providing a public platform for the community,
Addams believed that it was essential to use education to allow people
"outside the circle" to contribute their skills to the common lot. Thus,
settlements had a unique place in the ecology of civic learning. Addams
saw universities as places of research that developed new knowledge,
while colleges were places that passed that knowledge down. Settlements,
on the other hand, had the function of including men and women who
might otherwise be disenfranchised. And while Addams did this from
outside the university, she was in constant conversation with schools and
institutions of higher education.

Addams served on many educational commissions and boards, including a committee to improve the schools in 1893 and as a reformer on
the Chicago school board from 1905 to 1909. Addams also lectured regularly at the University of Chicago and the University of Wisconsin, and
welcomed faculty and students to join with Hull House in carrying out
research on poverty, working conditions, and health issues in Chicago.
But Addams resisted all attempts to get her to join any university, and
remained at Hull House her entire life.[59]

This unwillingness to join a university grew out of her understanding
of the unique role that settlements could play in the creation of knowledge by being centered in the community. "As the college changed from
teaching theology to teaching secular knowledge the test of its success
should have shifted from the power to save men's souls to the power
to adjust them in healthful relations to nature and their fellow men,"
Addams wrote. "But the college failed to do this, and made the test of
its success the mere collecting and disseminating of knowledge, elevat-
ing the means into an end and falling in love with its own achievement."[60] She then contrasted the settlement with the university, believing
that the settlement stands for "application as opposed to research; for
emotion as opposed to abstraction; for universal interest as opposed
to specialization."[61]

For Addams, who believed so strongly in the significance of narrative,
any institution that gave itself over to research, abstraction, and special-

ization was an institution that failed to support democracy. She also worried that the university would "swallow the settlement and turn it into one more laboratory: another place in which to analyze and depict, to observe and record."[62] Addams, therefore, strongly resisted attempts to have the settlement taken over by the University of Chicago, choosing instead to stay an autonomous educational partner, outside formal schooling.

This persistence in shifting the social center of education has had an influence on contemporary educational institutions. Ira Harkavy and John Puckett describe how the "settlement idea" inspired their efforts at the University of Pennsylvania to rethink the role the university could play in its surrounding community. Hull House was an ideal model for their efforts in Philadelphia because it "provided, albeit on a small neighborhood scale, a comprehensive institutional response to social problems."[63] The University of Pennsylvania has since become a national leader for campus–community–school partnerships using this model to advance knowledge, student learning, and community well-being. Harkavy and Puckett write that the key challenge today is: "to have universities function as perennial, deeply rooted settlements, providing illuminating space for their communities as they conduct their mission of producing and transmitting knowledge to advance human welfare and to develop theories that have broad utility and application."[64]

Freeing the Powers

In its role facilitating learning centered in the community, Hull House's educational philosophy was based on an unshakable belief in the powers of ordinary people, young and old. Trust in people was consequently a guiding principle. The role of the settlement worker was like that of a community educator unleashing people's greater possibilities. "We are gradually requiring of the educator that he shall free the powers of each man and connect him with the rest of life," Addams writes. "We ask this not merely because it is the man's right to be thus connected, but because we have become convinced that the social order cannot afford to get along without his special contribution."[65]

Addams's conception of education went beyond simply thinking about individual achievement; instead she thought about how education could help people contribute their talents and energies to a common, public life. "The strength of the settlement approach to education was that it taught young people to put theory into action applied to practical problems," write Harry Boyte and Nan Kari. "Settlement workers learned to work with immigrants in a reciprocal fashion. In this sense, settlement houses were a sort of citizenship school that created multiple opportunities for public work."[66]

This public approach—as opposed to notions of "helping the less fortunate"—is clear in Addams's writings. In "The Subtle Problems of Charity," Addams critiques charitable notions often associated with the work of the settlements and conveys disappointment in their inability to overcome these charitable assumptions.[67]

In her most articulate statement on the educational underpinnings of the settlement house idea, "A Function of the Social Settlement," Addams argues for its unique role in education. She defines settlements as an attempt to express the meaning of life in terms of life itself, in forms of activity. Settlements, she argues, combine theory and practice with a special interest in the *use* of an idea. Thus, Addams is critical of detached learning and knowledge for its own sake.

Addams also offers a timeless critique of the "not quite ready" assumptions that stifle the civic growth of young people when she writes, "A settlement would avoid the always getting ready for life which seems to dog the school, and would begin with however small a group to really accomplish and live." She continues that this always "getting ready for," rather than doing, unfortunately can easily be carried forward into life after graduation.[68]

Aware of the importance of making activities experiential, engaging, and relevant, Hull House offered a different approach. "In spite of the success of these Sunday evening courses, it has never been an easy undertaking to find acceptable lecturers," Addams notes about public lectures at Hull House. She continues by critiquing detached professional practice with a keen sense that learning needed to be practical, especially for adult learners. "The habit of research and the desire to say the latest word upon any subject often overcomes the sympathetic understanding of his audience which the lecturer might otherwise develop, and he insensibly drops into the dull terminology of the classroom."[69]

Hull House used what Paulo Freire would later term "a problem posing approach" with adult learners, calling on teachers to base their lessons on the experiences and problems of their foreign-born students.[70] Addams believed that "in order to do this the teachers must themselves acquire an understanding of those problems."[71]

One problem, according to Addams, was the lack of commitment to making the promise of democracy really mean participation by all people. In its mediating role, a settlement house engaged those who were not being invited into the democratic process. "We have learned to say that the good must be extended to all of society before it can be held secure by any one person or any one class," Addams tellingly writes about how they acted as educators for democracy and social justice. "But we have not yet learned to add to that statement, that unless all men and all classes contribute to a good, we cannot even be sure it is worth having."[72]

The Labor Museum: Valuing the Talents
of Immigrants

In perhaps Hull House's most deliberate and concrete example of its educational philosophy, Hull House created the Labor Museum in November 1900. Addams conceived of the plan for the Labor Museum, according to her autobiography, during an early morning walk around the neighborhood when she saw an Italian woman spinning thread using the primitive form of spindle reminiscent of those used in southern Europe. This woman represented, to Addams, the many Italian women living to the east of Hull House who in Italy spun and wove a family's entire wardrobe. Thus, she decided to develop an "educational enterprise" with educational as well as political results.

After discussions with John Dewey and a resident of Hull House who was also a teacher at Dewey's Laboratory School, Addams formulated her plan for the Labor Museum. The Labor Museum was marketed, even in its name, to capture the attention of adult learners. They decided to use "museum" rather than "school" because they felt school would be distasteful to adult learners because of its association with childish tasks, while the word museum still retained some fascinations of "the show."

The Labor Museum was an attempt to address the countervailing trends of cultural loss for new Americans and the alienating labor that resulted from an increasingly industrialized society. It was also an educational program, with grand political goals.

The Labor Museum began with a simple plan: to employ elder immigrants as teachers of their crafts to the next generation. The simple idea, however, had ambitious goals: to provide the older generation with meaningful work; to put the talents of the immigrants' home country to practical use at Hull House; to allow people to see the historical connections of their labor; and to distill a sense of pride in their cultural heritage to children struggling between American and immigrant identities. This was done through experiential, intergenerational training in the crafts of elder immigrants; it emphasized the resources of labor; and, Addams said, quoting Dewey, it conceived of education as a "continuing reconstruction of experience."[73]

Addams quotes workers as saying, "I was a glass blower in Vienna, but of course nobody wants such work in Chicago," and adds her hope that the Labor Museum would "offer at least the space, tools, and materials to men who care to work in them, and are but a feeble beginning toward restoring some balance between the attainment of various sorts of people."[74]

The original plan conceived of five departments, but lack of space and funding caused the Labor Museum to begin with a focus on textiles, with classes meeting every Saturday night. These courses in spinning and weaving soon expanded to include offerings in bookbinding, pottery-making, wood carving, and breadmaking. By 1903, classes were in progress every afternoon and evening and several mornings each week. The teachers had apprentices and sold their work to the public, which included hand weaves, such as rugs, towels, laces, embroideries, and baskets, as well as pottery, metal work, textiles, and woodwork. The demand for orders soon outstripped worker capacity to fill them.[75]

Hull House also connected the Labor Museum with its other programs—another example of an ecological approach to education. The Labor Museum, for example, connected with classes at Hull House, such as sewing, basket weaving, and dressmaking; students in the music school learned labor songs from early textile workers; and Hull House soon began a lecture series, which attracted as many as 350 people per lecture, on economic issues associated with the products created through the Labor Museum that connected the past and present.[76]

In describing the Labor Museum, as was her style, Jane Addams liked to use stories for translating experiences that are not easily transferred to audiences. Addams most liked to tell the story of Angelina discovering the talents of her mother—and her own heritage.

> I recall a certain Italian girl who came every Saturday evening to a cooking class in the same building in which her mother spun in the Labor Museum exhibit; and yet Angelina always left her mother at the front door because she did not wish to be too closely identified in the eyes of the rest of the cooking class with an Italian woman who wore a kerchief over her head, uncouth boots, and short petticoats. One evening, however, Angelina saw her mother surrounded by a group of visitors [teachers] from the School of Education [of the University of Chicago], who much admired the spinning, and she concluded from their conversation that her mother was 'the best stick-spindle spinner in America.' When she inquired from me as to the truth of this deduction, I took occasion to describe the Italian village in which her mother had lived, something of her free life, and how, because of the opportunity she and the other women of the village had to drop their spindles over the edge of a precipice, they had developed a skill in spinning beyond that of the neighboring towns. . . . It was easy to see that the thought of her mother with any other background than that of the tenement was new to Angelina and at least two things resulted; she allowed her mother to pull out of the big box under the bed the beautiful homespun garments which had been previously hidden away as uncouth; and she openly came into the Labor Museum by the same door as did her mother, proud at least of the mastery of the craft which had been so much admired.[77]

This is not the only powerful narrative Addams relates about the Labor Museum. For instance, in one of many other narratives, she tells of a group of some thirty Russian immigrants who stopped by Hull House one evening unexpectedly. When they arrived at the Labor Museum, they were instantly engaged. It connected them back to their lives in Russia. The Russians tried out the spindles and told stories of their home country. This experience put these immigrants in the position of leaders and teachers, a position they too seldom occupied in their new country. Addams observed that they began to "be the entertainers, rather than the entertained, to take the position which was theirs by right of much experience and long acquaintance with life."[78]

Giving immigrant culture a position on center stage was (and is) often ignored by American industrial and educational systems. Addams harshly criticized the "stupid way of trying to Americanize" immigrants, and concluded that teachers need to learn about the historical background of their students families and "meet the children on a common ground" so that they do not allow children to lose their heritage and love of their parents. This common ground was the community space created by Hull House.[79]

The Labor Museum, on the other hand, is an early example of what Harry Boyte calls "public work," with a diverse group of people in a common effort of public significance. This involves seeing education as more than workforce preparation; it entails seeing the civic implications of work. A visiting journalist wrote of the then four-year-old experiment: "The Museum stands for just this—for an attempt to change the common desire to make money into a desire to make useful things and make them well."[80]

But, at its core, the Labor Museum made real the mantra: "everyone is a teacher, everyone is a learner." Addams writes, "We prize it because it so often puts the immigrants into the position of teachers, and we imagine that it affords them a pleasant change from the tutelage in which all Americans, including their own children, are so apt to hold them."[81]

It is not entirely clear what became of the Labor Museum. Records from the Jane Addams Papers indicate that between $1,325 and $1,665 was spent on the Labor Museum each year from 1926 to 1934 for supplies such as textiles. Shortly after the death of Addams, the lead teacher was fired.[82] Furthermore, new residents viewed programs like the Labor Museum as out of date by the mid 1930s. The program, it seems, simply faded away. And yet, while the Labor Museum—and Hull House, more generally—did not achieve its most ambitious goals of overcoming the forces of industrialized labor, it does provide a powerful example of public work, democratic education, and intergenerational learning.

Conclusion

In one of her many descriptive narratives, Addams tells the story of a young girl who discovers a small toad in her mother's garden looking lonely. Like Addams herself, prior to founding Hull House, the girl felt the desire to contribute, but did not know how. Addams writes:

> Later in the day, quite at the other end of the garden, she found a large toad, also apparently without family and friends. With heart full of tender sympathy, she took a stick and by exercising infinite patience and some skill, she finally pushed the little toad through the entire length of the garden into the company of the big toad, when, to her surprise, the toad opened his mouth and swallowed the little one. The moral of the tale was clearly applied to people who lived "where they did not naturally belong," although I protested that was certainly what we wanted—to be swallowed and digested, to disappear into the bulk of the people.
>
> Twenty years later I am willing to testify that something of the sort does take place after years of identification with an industrial community.[83]

Many years after writing this story and an even greater distance from the day she moved into the giant house on Halsted Street, Jane Addams died on May 21, 1935. A Nobel Prize winner who received honorary doctorates and countless awards and honors, Addams was beloved and sometimes hated. She was an advocate for the most vulnerable; she nominated a president of the United States and fought for international peace. But even after more than forty-five years, Jane Addams was still a resident of Hull House.

Jane Addams and Hull House started by doing education in the community, but soon connected those efforts with the many political reform movements of the Progressive Era. Addams's Hull House inspired many to connect learning in the community with civic engagement, including Myles Horton and the founding of the Highlander Folk School—the case study to which I now turn.

Chapter Four

Highlander Folk School

I can remember one time when [Jane Addams and I] talked about this business of democracy and I asked her, "Well, what do you think democracy means?" She said, "It means people have the right to make decisions. If there is a group of people sitting around a country store and there's a problem they're talking about, there are two ways to do it. They can go out and get some official to tell them what to do, or they can talk it out and discuss it themselves. Democracy is if they did it themselves." I asked her where she got that idea, and she said she heard it from her father, who was a friend of Abraham Lincoln. I told her I didn't think that was bad advice at all.

—Myles Horton, *The Long Haul*

Prior to founding the Highlander Folk School in 1932 in the poor, rural area near the small Cumberland Plateau town of Monteagle, Tennessee, Myles Horton, like Jane Addams in the late nineteenth century, spent time researching and visiting examples of innovative approaches to education. Horton was looking for a way to put his hopes for social justice through democratic education into practice. These early inquiries brought him to Chicago to learn from, among other people, Jane Addams and her then forty-year experiment with community-based civic learning at Hull House. These visits gave Horton firsthand lessons from Addams on the early days at Hull House and her experiences with keeping its vision intact through difficult times. Most important, Horton came away inspired by the key similarity between Addams and himself: an abiding faith in democracy, along with an understanding of democracy as something you do.

During its first thirty years, Highlander was the education center for several social movements. It was a community folk school that was a training center for southern unions in the 1930s and 1940s, and a gathering place and partner for black and white civil rights activists in the 1950s and 1960s. Jane Addams and Hull House had an important influence on its approach to connect education with civic life.

Myles Horton and Jane Addams

Late in his life, Myles Horton recounted his meetings with Jane Addams and other residents of Hull House. These accounts could possibly be seen as exaggerations by a charismatic and savvy storyteller trying to connect his efforts with the more well-known work done at Hull House for dramatic effect. However, a private letter from Horton to Dr. Alice Hamilton seems to confirm otherwise—namely, that the impact of Hull House on Highlander was, in fact, genuine.

Alice Hamilton, a close colleague of Jane Addams who helped found the League of Nations, was honored for her research on workers' health in mines and factories; she also lived at Hull House for many years. After a *New York Times* article in February 1969 reported on the 100th birthday celebration of this remarkable woman, Horton wrote a note of congratulations. Horton begins, "Your fruitful and exciting life has been so packed with exciting people and causes that I do not expect you to remember me or the Highlander Folk School which you and Jane Addams contributed to in its prenatal stage." Horton then recalls Addams's reaction to his early ideas:

> When I was at the University of Chicago in 1930–31, I had the rare privilege of discussing my embryonic ideas a number of times with you and Jane Addams at the dinner table. Later she was to describe Highlander as a "rural settlement house reminiscent of the pioneer days of Hull House."[1]

Horton proceeds to describe to Hamilton the changes occurring at Highlander, explaining that Highlander was bringing on new, younger staff as they directed their efforts away from the civil rights movement and toward the rural poverty in the area surrounding Highlander in Appalachia. With these changes, Horton writes, the staff would take on more of the administrative duties, allowing him to focus on what he loved best: Highlander's educational mission. Horton then connects the work at Hull House and Highlander to future efforts in which community learning would be central to addressing social and economic problems. Horton writes: "Hopefully, I can help provide a bridge between the ideas we discussed at Hull House and the educational approaches that will have to be developed if today's social and economic problems are to be dealt with constructively."[2]

Horton speaks elsewhere about the time he spent in Chicago with Jane Addams and the inspiration and connections that came from this relationship. In an interview with biographer Frank Adams and then in his autobiography, *The Long Haul,* written with Herb and Judith Kohl, Horton describes his visits to Hull House. By arrangement, three or four students from the University of Chicago would go to Hull House for dinner with Addams and other Hull House residents. Horton explains the initial encounter with Addams, along with his interest in learning about the early days at Hull House, as follows:

> They seated us at a big table and went around asking why we had come to visit. Almost all of us said we were interested in social work and the great things they were doing at Hull House and so on. When my turn came, I just said what was on my mind. "Well, I'm not really interested in what's going on here now, but I'm terribly interested in how the place got started, the early struggles and how you dealt with the problem when you were put in jail, and what happened when you were branded Communists."[3]

The precocious Horton was concerned that he had hurt the feelings of the settlement house pioneers, admitting, it "was a tactless thing to say." A few minutes later, however, someone came over and told him that Miss Addams wanted to speak with him privately. Horton recalls, "I thought, 'Well, she's going to tell me off.'" His apprehension, however, proved unnecessary.

> When I got up there she said, "Why did you say that?" I told her that I was trying to think through what to do and wanted to know how to get things started. She asked me right there what I had in mind. She said it sounded as if I wanted to start a rural settlement house like Hull House. I said, "No, no, if it could be like you had at the beginning here, fine, but I don't want it to be like it is now." She laughed and said, "Maybe you'd better come down here when we have longer to talk," and she invited me back many times.[4]

Based on Horton's accounts, in these visits they discussed the founding of Hull House, the harassment Addams and others experienced because of the unpopular views they had taken on the war and women's rights, and the struggle to stay committed to the ideals of Hull House even when there was pressure to conform to broader undemocratic tendencies.[5] Each of these lessons would prove invaluable for the founding of Highlander and for getting through the turbulence that Highlander's populist educational approach encountered in the segregated South.

Myles Horton was deeply grateful to Addams for helping him think through his own ideas about democracy and education, proudly acknowledging that Addams's interest in Highlander continued until her death, shortly after Highlander was founded. Addams also helped connect Horton to other key leaders in the settlement house movement. For instance, Horton met with settlement pioneers from New York, such as Lillian Wald of Henry Street Settlement House and Mary Simkhovitch of Greenwich House, because of his relationship with Hull House. These relationships helped guide some of the early work at Highlander.[6]

Horton later describes the similarities and differences between what he envisioned for his rural folk school and the settlement house movement. Addams understood his rough ideas immediately, he wrote in his letter to Dr. Hamilton, observing what he had in mind was a "rural settlement, not a school." Horton agreed with this analysis, but reflected, "I always thought in terms of an *educational* program which would use some of the techniques of settlement houses."[7] Jane Addams would agree with this description, I'd imagine, but not only for Highlander. As I argued in the last chapter, this is consistent with the work of Hull House. Hull House, like Highlander, used learning in the community as a vehicle for democratic practice.

We can only imagine the impact the discussions with Jane Addams had on the young Myles Horton, eager to find practical ideas for the school he was hoping to start. These visits occurred prior to Horton's trip to Denmark, where he visited the Danish folk schools, which would further cement the ideas for Highlander. Apparent from Horton's recollection of the interactions with Addams was his interest in learning about the beginnings of Hull House, including the lessons for starting a new type of educational institution—one rooted in the community. Moreover, Horton was keenly aware that if he was successful, he would need to overcome the temptations to institutionalize and abandon the school's organic spirit. Because he wanted to connect education with social reform, he also prepared for attacks that would come from those interested in maintaining the status quo.

Learning about the early days at Hull House helped inspire Horton simply to start the school without having fixed ideas on the end results. On Christmas night, 1931, while visiting the Danish folk schools, several months after meeting with Jane Addams, Myles Horton wrote to himself:

> I can't sleep but there are dreams. What you must do is go back . . . get a simple place [and] move in. . . . The situation is there . . . you start with this and let it grow. . . . It will build its own structure and take its own form. You can go to school all your life and you'll never figure it out because you're trying to get an answer that can only come from people in the life situation.[8]

Almost one year after writing these words, Horton found the place and people to begin, and on November 1, 1932—just over forty-three years after the founding of Hull House—the Highlander Folk School was launched in Gundy Country, Tennessee, with the goal of linking education and social change.

No Ordinary School: Highlander

Myles Horton followed his own words of advice by simply "starting and letting it grow" and he helped Highlander grow in many shapes and forms, where it continues to flourish today. Like Addams at Hull House, Horton was active in the educational work at Highlander for what he described as "the long haul." In fact, Horton lived and worked at Highlander for more than fifty-eight years, until his death in 1990.

The history of Highlander has been well documented in several biographies, including historian John Glen's *Highlander: No Ordinary School*,[9] Aimee Horton's *The Highlander Folk School*,[10] and Frank Adams's *Unearthing Seeds of Fire*.[11] It has also been detailed in autobiographies by Myles Horton and Septima Clark;[12] a conversation book with Paulo Freire, *We Make the Road by Walking*;[13] and an edited collection of the writings of Myles Horton, *The Myles Horton Reader*.[14] This contribution, however, has been largely overlooked in the history of education. For instance, Lawrence Cremin only makes one brief mention of Highlander in his comprehensive history of American education.[15] Nevertheless, Highlander provides an impressive example for the ecology of civic learning.

The inspiration for Highlander came in multiple forms. Along with the influences of Hull House, Horton was shaped by the writings of John Dewey, his time studying with Robert Park at the Department of Sociology at the University of Chicago, and his courses with Reinhold Neibuhr at Union Theological Seminary in New York. Another significant influence was the Danish folk schools, conceived of by Bishop Nikolaj Grundtvig.[16]

The folk schools gave Horton a model with many of the foundational characteristics of Highlander. For instance, Highlander utilized the practices of students and teachers living together, engaging in peer-to-peer learning, and participating in fun activities, such as group singing and other social interactions over the course of a workshop. In addition, the Danish folk schools showed Horton that noncredentialized learning with adults could work, especially when learning took place within the context of a larger purpose. Horton left Denmark eager to initiate a folk school in his home state of Tennessee.

Upon his return from Denmark, Horton teamed with Don West and, soon thereafter, James Dombrowski to found Highlander near Monteagle,

Tennessee, on property provided by Lillian Johnson, a former professor at the University of Tennessee. Highlander was not the only folk school in the United States. Others included the John C. Campbell Folk School and Black Mountain, both in rural North Carolina. However, based on its community impact, sustainability, and connection to larger movements, it certainly must be viewed as the most successful.

Highlander, again like Addams's Hull House, was the creation of its founder's experiences with people in problem-based, situational learning. Highlander was an example of someone finding "vocational work." For Horton, this involved a practical model that connected education for the poor with democratic social transformation.

Horton's own beliefs had a significant influence on the shape of Highlander, as one might imagine. For instance, the noncredentialized ideas of Highlander were very much in the spirit of how Horton himself learned. During the time he spent studying at Union Theological Seminary and the University of Chicago, Horton's goal was never to obtain a degree; he hoped instead that these experiences would prepare him to put his educational ideas into practice when he returned to Tennessee.

Because of its unique approach to education, Highlander received high praise, even in its early days. For instance, John Dewey, the most famous philosopher of education in the world by the 1930s, was an early contributor to Highlander of both advice and money. Highlander complemented Dewey's interest in wider educational applications that linked community and democracy. In 1933, Dewey wrote a letter of endorsement to Highlander staff member James Dombrowski after a visit, stating that he was "much impressed with the intelligent sincerity and devotion of the plan and those who are engaged in carrying it out." He went to praise Highlander as "one of the most hopeful social-educational plans I know of."[17]

Dewey continued to support the educational developments at Highlander. In 1940, he wrote that Highlander was "making a considerable contribution to democratic institutions" through its education work with the organized labor movement—a movement that he believed was "of the most important, if not the most important, bulwark of democracy"—in a letter to the editor in the *Nashville Banner*.[18]

Highlander also had other well-known supporters, including former first lady Eleanor Roosevelt, civil rights legend Martin Luther King Jr., and the father of community organizing, Saul Alinsky. And Highlander's support for the civil rights movement continues to garner praise today. For example, when African American scholar Cornel West was asked to name the white person most sympathetic to changing the politics of racial difference in the United States, he named Myles Horton, whom he called "an incredibly courageous and visionary white brother from Tennessee."[19]

Highlander was at the center of several social movements and struggles for social justice, most notably the labor movement in the 1930s and 1940s and the civil rights movement in the 1950s and 1960s. During this time, it operated under two different charters. The Highlander Folk School's charter, located fifty miles northeast of Chattanooga, Tennessee, near a little town called Monteagle on 200 acres of land along rolling hills covered with trees on the Cumberland Plateau, lasted from 1932 to 1962. Like a modern-day college campus—in this case, a rural campus—it consisted of fourteen buildings used for conferences, recreation, dormitories, offices, and living space for staff.

After the original charter was revoked by the state of Tennessee because of Highlander's support for desegregation, Highlander Folk School officially became Highlander Research and Education Center and temporarily relocated in Knoxville, Tennessee. It continues to operate today in a beautiful new location in New Market, Tennessee.[20]

The success of Highlander must be seen partly in the vision and skills of Horton—a charismatic leader who was able to listen and learn from others. However, the communities and community leaders, along with the Highlander staff, had the most profound impact on the school's learning approach and direction. Highlander was a cocreation of the people who participated. These leaders helped Highlander adapt to changing times, issues, and circumstances.

Like Hull House, Highlander helped develop and utilize the talents of an amazing assortment of community leaders. In addition to West and Dombrowski, long-time staff members included Septima Clark and Bernice Robinson, who organized in southern black communities, and Guy and Candie Carawan, who led the music programming. Highlander's "students" included such civil rights leaders, as Fannie Lou Hamer, Ella Baker, John Lewis, Bob Moses, Diane Nash, and James Bevel. The most famous student to attend workshops at Highlander was Rosa Parks, who attended her first workshop just prior to initiating the Montgomery bus boycott on December 1, 1955.

Rosa Parks is worth mentioning because her experience illuminates the subtle transformative power of democratic education. In the last workshop session at Highlander in the summer of 1955, Parks admitted she didn't know what she could do when she got home "in the cradle of the Confederacy."[21] However, she later connected her experiences at Highlander with the contributions she made to help catalyze the civil rights movement. "At Highlander, I found out for the first time in my adult life that this could be a unified society, that there was such a thing as people of differing races and backgrounds meeting together in workshops and living together in peace and harmony," says Parks, who was executive secretary of the NAACP in Montgomery at the time of the workshop. "It was a place I was very reluctant to leave. I gained there strength to persevere in my work for freedom, not just for Blacks, but for all oppressed people."[22]

The story of Rosa Parks is not simply the story of a civil rights hero getting trained at Highlander. Rather, it is also a story of the educational philosophy of Highlander in action. Highlander cultivated an atmosphere that allowed people to find their own voice and put it to use on issues that mattered most to them. One would assume, for example, that the workshop Parks attended was on civil disobedience or boycott strategies. It was not. Rather, the workshop she attended was on school desegregation, on strategies for implementing the 1954 *Brown v. Board of Education* Supreme Court decision outlawing segregated public schooling. As Horton often reminded people, "The best ways of educating people is to give them an experience that embodies what you are trying to teach. When you believe in a democratic society, you provide a setting for education that is democratic."[23] This community-based, democratic education allowed Parks, and countless others during the civil rights movement, to experience the possibility of a desegregated society. It led her to act on her conviction with greater experiences that confirmed her hopes for integration and democracy.

Highlander also cultivated the civic leadership of thousands of young people through its extensive partnerships with college students and institutions of higher education. Highlander conducted annual college workshops beginning in 1954 and continuing through 1961. These workshops provided black and white college students with leadership training to eliminate racial discrimination and fight for civil rights. The colleges involved included Fisk University, Morehouse College, Emory University, the University of Texas, the University of Tennessee, and many others. Highlander also worked closely with the Student Non-Violent Coordinating Committee (SNCC) and hosted many of their workshops and trainings. And Septima Clark and others on staff conducted workshops solely for white college students on the role of students in the changing South.[24]

Highlander was also sometimes asked to play a mediating role between college students and community members in the civil rights movement. Conflict inevitably arose between students and their host communities as residents became concerned about the tactics utilized by college students that included disobeying the law and going to jail; community members also rightly questioned the long-term commitment of students who came to their communities for weekend marches and community organizing during summer breaks. Community members asked pointed questions about what would happen after the students left town. To address these concerns, as was their way, Highlander staff used dialogue and deliberation to overcome conflict. Highlander staff, for instance, coordinated and facilitated a series of workshops between students and community leaders at which they could build more trusting relationships and overcome these conflicts.

These activities led to a series of fierce criticisms of Highlander. Highlander had many powerful enemies, which led to its charter getting revoked in 1962—and its reopening in a new location in Tennessee. By its critics and people who knew it only by its reputation, Highlander was branded "a communist training school." One persistent critic, a U.S. senator from Mississippi, described Highlander as a "front for a conspiracy to overthrow this country."[25]

More recent critics point out that Highlander did not directly tackle gender discrimination. They observe that Highlander was slow to see the power of youth as agents of change, as Horton was even hesitant to work with the student organizers at SNCC until young leaders began to get arrested at demonstrations. Critics also note that Highlander never realized its vision—at least not yet—of creating many Highlander-type people's institutions throughout the United States.[26]

Over the course of its history, Highlander had many periods of transition, times when it was finding its way from one movement to the next. In 1953, for example, Highlander received a grant to "train community leaders." Highlander was transitioning out of its work with labor unions and searching for the next phase in its social change efforts.

This era of exploration—what Horton has termed "valley" periods—allowed for "peak" periods during the labor movement and civil rights movement. The period following 1953 of experimenting with community leadership training ultimately led to the creation of the Citizenship Schools and Highlander's deep involvement in the civil rights movement. During this time between social movements, Highlander attempted to lay the foundation so that it was on the inside when a movement occurred. Highlander staff built relationships, listened to people, honed their techniques, and improved their ability to involve people in solving their own problems. These foundations are embodied in the educational philosophy and practices of Highlander summed up by Horton: "Our whole approach to life is an educational approach."[27]

Circle of Learners

The heart of the educational approach practiced by Highlander, as at Hull House, involves trusting in people. Horton explains:

> When Highlander workshops are described to people who haven't experienced them, it often sounds like we are always contradicting ourselves, because we do things differently every time, according to what is needed. We've changed methods and techniques over the years, but the

philosophy and conditions for learning stay the same. There is no
method to learn from Highlander. What we do involves trusting people
and believing in their ability to think for themselves.[28]

Trusting in people meant investing time and energy in the individuals, groups, and communities that Highlander worked with. These in-
vestments paid great dividends—and tended to be reciprocated. Rosa
Parks, for example, reflected that Myles Horton was the first white man
she ever trusted and that he taught her that it was possible to trust other
white people.[29]

This basic trust undergirded all of Highlander's efforts. At one time
Highlander considered initiating a community school for all ages, infus-
ing its educational philosophy into traditional education, but that plan
never materialized. Highlander's aim has instead been to work with people and communities for social justice outside traditional educational institutions. Highlander tried to find people with common concerns, invite
them to talk through their problems in a safe environment, and then discover methods for solving these problems through a democratic exchange of ideas. Horton argued with organizer Saul Alinsky for many
years about an *educational* approach versus an organizing one.[30]

The deliberate educational approach that allowed Highlander to put
problem-based learning at the core was the workshop method with a "circle of learners."[31] "I think of an educational workshop as a circle of learners," Horton writes. "'Circle' is not an accidental term, for there is no
head of the table at Highlander workshops; everybody sits around a circle."[32] Out of this description, others, including John Wallace of the University of Minnesota, have termed the style of teaching and learning at
Highlander "learning circles."[33]

Learning circles at Highlander were ideally suited for longer periods
of time with at least one day when no one was traveling (leaving or arriving). Myles Horton was adamant about the importance of this type of
time for group continuity and trusting relationships to develop. Moreover, the learning circles often lasted much longer, sometimes as long as
several weeks. Workshops were intensive, around-the-clock experiences
of living and learning in community. Horton believed that "a person who
has been to a Highlander session at Highlander is several times more effective than a person with whom a Highlander staff person has worked
only in his own community." Horton continued: "There is something
about the experience of living and working together and being closely associated without outside distractions for a period of days or weeks which
heightens the educational process."[34]

In describing what happens during this heightened educational process, Horton, unknowingly, gives one of the best definitions of education in the community:

> Learning in society, outside school walls, takes place around the clock. It isn't restricted to specific times, certainly not to the same time of day for a limited number of minutes for, say, math, and then to another block of time for another subject. That's not life. Some of the best education at Highlander happened when the sessions were over: at meals, on walks, and when people went back to their dormitories and sat around drinking coffee or whatever else they brought.[35]

Highlander workshops were based on "mining" the experiences that participants brought with them. The core ingredient for any learning circle is the idea that experiences are co-created, based on people's stories. Conversation begins where people are, and then grows out of these experiences. Horton wanted participatory, active learners, not what Paulo Freire calls passive learners, who are simply asked to put information "into a bank" to be retrieved on command at a later date.[36] With this approach, small learning communities with deep and engaged relationships took precedence over larger, more passive groups; Horton believed this was the most effective strategy for connecting education with social change. For instance, Horton once tellingly wrote, "Twenty learners will eventually reach more people and be more effective than two hundred listeners."[37]

To convey this method of democratic education to others, Horton used several helpful metaphors. The most powerful was the idea of a "two-eyed theory of education." Horton's "two-eyed theory" recognizes the importance of respecting people's unique experiences, but also dreaming of the growth that might take place through the educational process. Thus, Horton asks educators to be aware of people's experiences, values, and identities—this is the first eye—and then use a second eye to see transformational possibility in the learning goals. Horton explains:

> I like to think that I have two eyes that I don't have to use the same way. When I do educational work with a group of people, I try to see with one eye where those people are as they perceive themselves to be. I do this by looking at body language, by imagination, by talking to them, by visiting them, by learning what they enjoy and what troubles them. I try to find out where they are, and if I can get hold of that with one eye, that's where I start. You have to start where people are, because their growth is going to be from there, not from some abstraction or where you are or someone else is.

Now my other eye is not such a problem, because I already have in mind a philosophy of where I'd like to see people moving. It's not a clear blueprint for the future but movement toward goals they don't conceive of at the time. . . . Then I set up a tension between where people are and where they can be, and I make people uncomfortable quite often because I keep pushing them, trying to help them grow.[38]

Horton also used other metaphors to describe the learning process, including comparing the learning process to a magnifying glass catalyzing a multitude of fires:

While the approach is diverse and kaleidoscopic, the focus (predetermined by the purpose or goal) is specific and must always be kept in mind. The process is like the use of a magnifying-glass to focus the sun's rays on a leaf and set it on fire, qualified with the knowledge that the results may be spread out over a period of years. The delay is compensated for the fact that once achieved it is multiplied.[39]

In a conversation with Paulo Freire, Horton uses another descriptive metaphor to explain how Highlander's theory of education involves more than people simply sitting in a circle, chatting, without any direction. Horton responds to this critique by comparing democratic education to planting a garden:

Someone criticized Highlander workshops, saying, "All you do is sit there and tell stories." Well, if he'd seen me in the spring planting my garden, he would've said: "That guy doesn't know how to grow vegetables. I don't see any vegetables.". . . Well he was doing the same thing about observing the workshop. It was the seeds getting ready to start, and he thought that was the whole process. To me it's essential that you start where people are. But if you're going to start where they are and they don't change, then there's no point in starting because you're not going anywhere. . . . But if you don't have some vision of what ought to be or what they can become, then you have no way of contributing anything to the process.[40]

One of Highlander's most successful seeds grew into the Citizenship Schools.

Before examining the Citizenship Schools, however, the practices that embody a learning circle at Highlander should be explored. Educators interested in creating learning communities cannot help being curious about what the inside of one of these well-prepared, but open-ended workshops looked like. It would be invaluable for education for democracy today by helping to explain the praxis of Highlander's theory and practice.

Planning a Workshop

In its educational practice, Highlander did not have a rigid, prescribed curriculum. Horton feared that overstructuring a workshop would damage the spirit of trust and creativity. Participants were the experts who would set the tone, the substance, and the direction for the discussions and collective action-planning. "In planning the program you make it flexible since the interests of the participants may change from day to day and cannot be anticipated," Horton noted. "Flexibility is more important than the plan."[41]

Many hours of planning, however, went into creating an atmosphere that cultivated spontaneous education. Horton explains the detailed planning process involved in preparing for a workshop:

> First you plan who will be in charge and give them a few ideas. Then you call in a few people to help you plan. At this planning session you arrive at a focus for the workshop by deciding what specific part of the overall subject could best be related to the people back in their communities. You discuss and plan and write down the actual daily schedule, the materials to be used, the physical set-up, etc. You select the right resource people who will fit the problems decided on, who have had experience in these problems, and can relate their experience to the individual problems of the participants. Plans are made for recruiting, financing, publicizing and definite responsibilities are given to those helping with the planning.[42]

In this process, Horton used a technique he perfected over the years of visualizing the soon-to-come workshop in his mind, thus making a movie of how things might go. He envisioned potential situations and when he found things that might go wrong, he'd re-edit the film in his mind, or start over. Then he'd replay potential scenarios until he was comfortable that he was well prepared for the inevitably unexpected.[43]

Workshop Sections

Although there was no set program or agenda, Horton does admit that the workshop often had three major sections. The first section allowed people to state and analyze their problems, on their own terms and in their own language, with and among their peers. Sitting in a circle, participants would tell stories and share their experiences. This most often happened in some variation of a circle "go around."

The next section involved having the Highlander staff play a more active role. The staff would provoke participants and attempt to shine new light on issues by introducing data, synthesizing participants' own experiences, and asking participants to reflect on their problems in new ways. "There might be some sound research that throws light on the problem which we can bring into the picture," Horton says. "Or there might be the experience of somebody else, or it might be something written in a book."[44]

The final section of a workshop was forward looking. It involved asking participants to discuss some variation of the question, "What are you going to do when you get back home?" Future actions were discussed in terms of participants' growth and realizations over the course of the workshop and the resources that were available to make change in their home communities.

The Facilitator

In a Highlander workshop the facilitator had a unique and important role. To use Horton's words, he or she was not a "fact regurgitator," but rather played the role of a facilitator of learning or a "learning demonstrator."[45] The use of questions was—and is—the simplest and most important tool the facilitator employed. Horton describes how during the course of group conversations many different issues arise that can take the conversation in different directions. When this happens, Horton argues, the facilitator must steer the conversation in the most useful direction through the use of "a question about something that seems of general interest that will focus the attention of the group."[46]

If the facilitator crafted the right set of questions that interested a group, Horton felt, "Even those who have talked about other things will relate to the discussion around the issue by the question." It is essential, however, that questions build on the conversations of the group so that "no one feels put upon or ignored since the discussion is based on something raised by their peers, and not injected."[47]

Methods

A number of methods were used to initiate discussions in Highlander workshops. The most common was a learning circle "go around" at which facilitators asked participants to share problems and experiences and then brainstorm ways to mobilize for action. During some workshops, Highlander employed panel discussions to expose a variety of ideas about a topic in a manner that was more interesting than a lecture, but faster than a discussion. Speakers were also sometimes invited to give speeches to inspire people, or when specific information was required, especially about experiences in solving problems. Speakers playing this role included civil rights leaders, such Martin Luther King Jr., and former first lady Eleanor Roosevelt, as well as local leaders.

The Highlander staff also used experiential methods. Theater and role-playing helped stimulate discussion, especially with young people. They used audiovisuals to present material. In addition, during workshops Highlander sometimes taped discussions. This served dual purposes: it allowed a group to review its conversations and also gave Highlander a record of the discussions.

Along with discussions, music, singing, and dancing were integral parts of the holistic method of education at Highlander. Zilphia Horton (Myles's first wife, who was active in Highlander programs until her death in April 1956), Guy and Candie Carawan, staff members for almost forty years who still participate in Highlander workshops, and frequent visitors Bernice Reagon and Sweet Honey in the Rocks, Woody Guthrie, and Pete Seeger provided music. Songs that Highlander helped popularize in the civil rights movement included "Keep Your Eyes on the Prize" and "We Shall Overcome."[48]

In addition to music, food was an essential and carefully crafted part of the workshop experience. Black and white participants prepared food together, ate together, and had snacks late into the night (before sleeping in integrated rooms), allowing learners to talk about their lives, informally, over dinner and before bed.

Finally, the atmosphere itself was conducive to a successful workshop. Highlander took people away from the chaos of their everyday lives and allowed them to reflect and learn in the midst of a beautiful mountain setting. This was by design and helped Highlander create the type of safe space for a different type of political education.

Citizenship Schools

The story of Highlander, especially the lessons learned for advancing the ecology of civic learning, are perhaps best captured in the story of the Citizenship Schools. The Citizenship Schools used the desire for literacy education and voter registration to create active and engaged citizens. The project also matched Highlander's interest in leadership trainings with the desire of the community of Johns Island to give black citizens political power by helping them gain the right to vote through literacy education.[49]

Esau Jenkins and Johns Island

The Citizenship Schools began to ferment under the leadership of Esau Jenkins, a social entrepreneur from Johns Island, one of the largest Sea Islands off the coast of Charleston, South Carolina. In the 1950s, Johns Island had a population of more than 6,000 people, a majority of whom were black residents who spoke with a Gullah dialect. Jenkins was a leader on the island. He was president of the PTA, superintendent of the Methodist Sunday School, assistant pastor of his church, president of the Citizens Club (a group concerned with community and school improvement), chairman of the Progressive Club (a group organized to give financial assistance to those in legal need), and a member of the executive board of the Charleston NAACP when he attended his first Highlander workshop in August 1954. Jenkins, a tireless promoter of civil rights, even ran, unsuccessfully, for the school board. He did, however, get 203 votes in his effort to illustrate the importance of getting more blacks registered. Not coincidentally, many of these institutions played a role within the ecology of civic learning for the Citizenship Schools. Furthermore, Jenkins's role as the owner and driver of several buses would also prove significant.

One morning on his bus, a woman heading toward Charleston described a problem common to many on the island and throughout the South. "I don't have much schooling, Esau," Mrs. Alice Wine explained. "I wasn't even able to get through the third grade. But I would like to be somebody. I'd like to hold up my head with other people; I'd like to be able to vote. Esau, if you'll help me a little when you have the time, I'll be glad to learn the laws and get qualified to vote. If I do, I promise you I'll register and I'll vote."[50] Jenkins was moved to act, making his bus the first site of the citizenship school idea. Jenkins began by typing up the section of the South Carolina laws that pertained to registration and voting and then helping his passengers study the requirements. Jenkins described the process:

> I would start for Charleston about 6:45 or 7:00 a.m. for those going to work at 8:00. . . . While driving, I would talk about definitions of words in the constitution of South Carolina, procedures relating to voting and voter registration. After arrival, we would hold class. Before registration days, we would do this two or three days per week.[51]

Jenkins was aware, however, that the Johns Island black community needed more than his bus trips to meet the voting requirements. Thus, he began to look for a permanent site where adults could learn to read and practice citizenship. This led him to the Highlander Folk School.

Jenkins had been to Highlander for several retreats. He originally came at the encouragement of Septima Clark, who knew him from when he was a child. After the local school and the Methodist Center were unwilling to support the project to educate local blacks to read for fear of getting involved, he turned to Highlander. Jenkins asked Septima Clark and Myles Horton if Highlander could partner with Johns Island on civic education.

As mentioned earlier, Highlander had been attempting to engage in "community leadership trainings" since the early 1950s. These efforts had been largely unsuccessful because of Highlander's inability to connect with local community leaders on their own terms. Furthermore, Highlander failed because it was trying to move too quickly, without spending enough time developing the relationships necessary to have the community own the outcomes of the trainings. The partnership with Johns Island, however, would be different.[52]

Over the next several years Highlander staff spent time visiting with and listening to the people of Johns Island. Septima Clark, who joined Highlander full-time in June 1956 after getting fired from her teaching job in Charleston because of her involvement in the local NAACP, recalls, "One Christmas Myles went down there with his children and spent the whole Christmas season just walking around the island and talking. He stayed in Esau's house, and the people really enjoyed him."[53] This was a successful strategy because "Myles had a way of speaking to people which made them become endeared to him," according to Clark.[54]

The connection with a community practitioner, such as Esau Jenkins, also had a dramatic impact. Jenkins enabled whites, such as Horton, and city blacks, such as Clark, to gain the trust of the secluded island community. Clark was well aware of the importance of having such a connector. "Esau could be trusted on the island, and because he could be trusted, he could introduce us to numbers of others who would trust us," explains Clark.[55]

After this time spent organizing, Highlander raised funds to provide a loan of $1,500 to Jenkins's Progressive Club to buy a building for the school. The building was renovated and became the site not only for the school, but also for a revenue-generating store. The front room became a grocery store, both to "fool white people" and to generate profits to pay for the school. Highlander also raised funds to hire a teacher.

The Right Teacher: Bernice Robinson

The next task was to find the right teacher, perhaps the most important decision the group would make. Horton, aware of the limits of professional expertise, didn't want a certified teacher because "people with teaching experience would likely impose their schooling methodology on the students and be judgmental."[56] With this in mind, Highlander recruited Septima Clark's cousin, Bernice Robinson, to be the first teacher on the island. Robinson had no training as a teacher. In fact, she was a beautician in New York who moved back to Charleston to be closer to her ill mother. Myles Horton explains:

> Bernice was a black beautician. Compared to white beauticians, black beauticians had status in their own community. They had a higher-than-average education and, because they owned their own business, didn't depend upon whites for their incomes. We needed to build around black people who could stand up against white opposition, so black beauticians were terribly important.[57]

At first Robinson was hesitant, "I'm a beautician. I don't know anything about teaching." But Clark and Horton were confident in her ability. Clark later explains, "We knew that she had the most important quality, the ability to listen to people."[58]

The selection of Robinson was consistent with Highlander's broader hiring philosophy. Highlander did not hire staff because of credentials; people were chosen based on commitment to social justice, knowledge of the communities they would be working with, and experience trying to empower others. Horton explains the staffing selection process in a memo:

> Highlander staff members are not selected because of adult education experience or because of their experience as teachers or discussion leaders. These things are readily learned. . . . Staff are people who are committed to the objectives of a designed program at a given time and have knowledge of the people for whom the program is designed and experience, good and bad, in trying to help them solve their problems. These things cannot be readily and rapidly learned.[59]

The First Class

After three months of planning, Robinson began the first class of fourteen adult students, along with thirteen high school girls enrolled to start sewing, in 1956 in the back room of the cooperative store by insisting on the theme that would epitomize the Citizenship Schools: everyone is a teacher and everyone is a learner. "I am not a teacher, we are here to learn together. You're going to teach me as much as I'm going to teach you."[60] She also respected the human dignity of the adult learners and placed the United Nations Declaration of Human Rights on the wall for them to eventually learn to read.

The curriculum for the first class evolved based on the desires of the students who participated. At the first meeting, for instance, Robinson found that the students were interested in learning how to write their names and the words from the South Carolina election laws. Three adults had to start from scratch because they could not read or write. Students were also interested in more practical pursuits, such as learning how to fill in blanks when ordering from a catalogue and how to complete a money order. During the initial sessions, Robinson asked the students to tell stories about things they did in their everyday lives, and then taught them to write their stories down.[61] Robinson describes the progress of this first group in a letter to Septima Clark:

> They really want to learn and are so proud of the little gains they have made so far. When I get to the club each night, half of them are already there and have their homework ready for me to see. I tacked up the Declaration of Human Rights on the wall and told them that I wanted each of them to be able to read and understand the entire thing before the end of the school.[62]

This class continued, in three-month intervals, with black students learning to read and then registering to vote. As word of the schools spread, so did demand.

Expansion

Interest in the Citizenship Schools grew throughout the Sea Island communities of Johns Island, Wadmalaw, North Area, Edisto Island, and Daufuskie.[63] Hundreds of people enrolled in these schools, learned to read, and registered to vote—becoming engaged citizens in the process. The results were impressive.

In 1958, for example, there were no blacks registered to vote on Wadmalaw Island. By 1973, more than 1,000 were registered. More important, the school helped create the infrastructure for black residents' civic engagement and social capital with the development of local organizations, such as the Board of Concerned Members of Wadmalaw Island.[64]

By 1960, the Citizenship Schools expanded beyond the Sea Islands to Savannah, Georgia, and Huntsville, Alabama. The original model of the first schools was kept: communities interested in initiating a school would send community leaders to a workshop at Highlander and then return to their home communities to start Citizenship Schools. There was also continuing assistance provided by the Highlander field staff, including Clark and Robinson.

With expansion also came important lessons. In a handwritten letter to Myles Horton, Septima Clark provides insight into the importance of local connections and the commitment of time. Clark compares the sites for Citizenship School expansion, Savannah and Huntsville, to the original locations in Charleston and the Sea Islands. "I was literally a Charlestonian and Sea Islander and knew the people on the islands and in the city," Clark writes. She continues that she was "known to them and trusted by them" and therefore she could "go to them with one potential leader and do a program."[65]

She compares the experience of having local ties with her experience with Huntsville, Alabama, and Savannah, Georgia, where she did not have previous relationships. In these places, she first met community leaders at Highlander and had to earn their trust. She explains that this required more time with potential leaders and forced her to "lean heavily" on "Highlander students in the community for support, for trust, and for faith in doing a program and not let them get the old feeling of exploiting them." Building this trust was even more important because of Highlander's reputation throughout the South as a "communist school." Clark explains, "They must learn to believe in me and not the adverse publicity that they read or hear about me and Highlander."[66]

Success in expansion also depended on the culture of a place and its openness to informal education. Colleges and universities often served as an obstacle to this nontraditional learning, and Horton was known to admit he had to "unlearn" things he learned in school. Septima Clark complained that the two colleges in Huntsville made the city "degree crazy" and, as a result, doing a program in Huntsville necessitated more financing, especially in the beginning. It required, in these settings, more effort for people to think expansively about education. Clark was optimistic, however, and concluded, "I know we can hammer on it but it takes constant hammering and I'm sure we'll need more financing than the islands in the beginning."[67]

Trainings to Catalyze Citizenship Schools

As the effectiveness of the Citizenship Schools became better documented, Highlander sent out an invitation to other organizations to make use of the idea. To support these other organizations, Highlander developed a training program for volunteer teachers and supervisors beginning in 1959, four years after the first class on Johns Island. This transformed Highlander's role from sponsorship and direct supervision of the program to acting as a catalyst that provided training to other sponsor organizations.

Training for these weeklong workshops included presentation of the citizenship school idea; a role-playing demonstration of the citizenship classes with reflection and critiques from the audience; skill-building activities (including how to operate tape recorders, record players, and film and slide projectors); instruction on class programming and educational activities; time for planning the arrangements for future classes (such as time and place for the class and recruitment strategies); and, of course, singing. The workshop also used films and speakers to broaden people's ideas about citizenship. And time was dedicated for personal reflection on participants' experiences with segregation and integration throughout the workshops.

The final activity encouraged participants to be forward-looking. The last session, like all Highlander workshops, asked participants to reflect on: "What are you going to do when you get back home?" Participants then discussed and presented their plans. This gave them a chance to "talk out" their ideas for clarity; get group feedback, suggestions, and support; and produce public commitments among their peers.[68]

During the trainings, participants used community mapping techniques, with questionnaires on their communities' backgrounds that included practical questions on what three-month period and hours would work best in participants' home communities, local voting and registration requirements, and potential community-based organizations and allies. Questions probing for problems teachers might encounter while trying to initiate community-based schools were also included, such as "What are some of your problems in getting the Citizenship School program started in your community?" and "What were problems of operation?" All of these prompts were used to initiate conversations and collective problem-solving.

Moving to the Southern Christian Leadership Conference

Even with these set questions, the learning at Highlander continued to happen in an organic way, coming from people's lived experiences. One important decision Highlander made, according to Horton, was to "stay small and not get involved in mass education or in education activities that required large amounts of money." He continued, "We solved the problem of staying small by spinning off programs that were already established and were willingly taken over by organizations less interested in creating new programs."[69]

These spin-offs enabled Highlander to concentrate on creating small, cutting-edge programs that no one else in the region was undertaking. This is what happened with the Citizenship School program.

With the training in place, the growth of the program, and the legal problems confronting Highlander from the state of Tennessee, Highlander began to search for a new sponsor. In February 1961, the Citizenship Schools found their sponsor: the Southern Christian Leadership Conference (SCLC), led by Martin Luther King Jr.

At first, King was reluctant to take over the program from Highlander, but he was lobbied by Clark, along with Ella Baker. The Citizenship Schools were also registering more people in the South than any SCLC programs, a point that wasn't lost to the pragmatic leader of the civil rights movement. Eventually, King and SCLC agreed. Aside from the training, SCLC also gained valuable staffing expertise from Highlander. In the summer of 1961, Septima Clark moved to SCLC and became their director of workshops, working with Andrew Young and Dorothy Cotton to greatly expand the Citizenship School program at SCLC.[70]

The program grew rapidly throughout the segregated South over the next few years. In a report to the Board of Directors of Highlander in 1965, Septima Clark noted that since leaving Highlander more than 25,000 people had taken classes and they were responsible for more than 50,000 registered voters. To accomplish this, 1,600 volunteer teachers from eleven southern states attended trainings at Dorchester Center in southern Georgia.[71]

Expansion, however, brought changes to the Citizenship School trainings. The SCLC put less emphasis on developing people and more focus on organizing a social movement. Training workshops grew larger, from twenty-five to forty-five people. This reduced the intimacy of the more interactive atmosphere that characterized the earlier efforts, but it also allowed SCLC to train more people. The workshops were also reduced from a full week to four days and a night. This was for practical purposes: it allowed people to participate in demonstrations sponsored by SCLC on the weekends. Omitted from the shortened workshop was the essential closing session exploring, "What are you going do when you get back home?"

Some were critical of the changes brought about with the transfer to SCLC, especially around the organization's ability to follow through with communities—something Highlander had made a priority. Partially because of the scale of their program, SCLC put less emphasis on the development of community partners. "Lack of follow-up was the great weakness," remarks Septima Clark. She continues, "But [Martin Luther] King never absorbed the lesson of what it took to make the citizenship education program work."[72] The omission of the final session eliminated much of the feelings of trust, solidarity, and commitment that were central to Highlander's approach. However, the Citizenship Schools under SCLC did still attempt to maintain an emphasis on teaching people how to set up Citizenship Schools in their home communities, even as they devoted less time toward this pursuit.

Others saw improvements in the program after it moved to SCLC. Harry Boyte and Nan Kari argue that the Citizenship Schools took on a more deliberate emphasis on political education. They interviewed Dorothy Cotton, director of the Citizenship Education Program for SCLC, who explains that under SCLC the citizenship program used the question "What is a citizen?" to frame its activities. There was also a focus on multiform civic engagement. The SCLC made efforts to connect the learning sessions more directly with the broader civil rights movement by integrating the classes with SCLC actions.[73]

Regardless of positive and negative changes, some lessons and results were evident through their various iterations. The Citizenship School program, like Highlander more broadly (and Hull House), used education in the community for democratic purposes. "The citizenship program was about teaching people to free themselves," says Cotton, in language reminiscent of Jane Addams's definition of education as "freeing the powers" of ordinary people. Cotton continues, "People learned new ways of functioning as they learned to think in different ways about themselves and each other." Cotton goes on to explain that "it's supposed to be 'government of the people, by the people, and for the people'—but it's *only true if you make it so*. They could no longer sit back and wait for someone else to do it."[74] In short, the Citizenship Schools put into practice the civil rights idea that "we are the ones we've been waiting for" as people learned new ways to gain political voice and power.

Conclusion

Carl Tjerandsen's research on the success of the Citizenship Schools illustrates the power of the ecology of civic learning. He points out that, as opposed to other communities in which Highlander had tried to provide community leadership training, Johns Island already had an organizational framework of sorts—an assortment of churches as well as clubs like the Citizens Club and the Progressive Club—through Esau Jenkins, an essential community connector. These institutions had untapped civic potential. The multitude of community organizations, according to Tjerandsen, was invaluable "as vehicles within which leadership training and education for civic competence could take place."[75]

The Citizenship Schools embody how Highlander promoted civic learning in a community setting. The schools showed how educational institutions can tap into other institutions to support community learn-ing for the development of what was then termed "first class citizenship." The democratic education at Highlander, like the settlement house movement, recalls a dramatic lesson: ordinary people, even people who are poor and uneducated in a formal sense and who suffered from long histories of abuse and oppression, can develop civic self-confidence and make lasting contributions to their communities.[76]

Highlander shows the promise of democratic education in the form of a circle of learners. In its beautiful, natural setting, citizens were given space to reflect and plan outside their home communities as a strategy for developing community leadership and promoting democratic prac-tices. This model put an abiding trust in people and in a democratic process that builds on people's cultures and stories. It shows the ability of nonprofessionals to contribute their talents. Highlander illustrates the power of working with people in communities at their request. And Myles Horton and Highlander demonstrate that partnerships works best when done in the context of working together over the long haul.

Highlander and Hull House conceptualized "place" in community differently from one another: Hull House was localized in an urban neighborhood, while Highlander used secluded, rural settings to build educative communities. However, both created remarkable projects that connected multiple institutions to educate for democracy. Like Hull House, Highlander has much to teach civic educators today. As Horton wrote to Alice Hamilton, these traditions are connected and can also serve as bridges to new civic learning initiatives, as seen in the following case study on the Neighborhood Learning Community.

Chapter Five

The Neighborhood
Learning Community

We're trying to create a community alive with learning.

—Nan Skelton

In neighborhoods across America, there is a great, often unrealized, potential for learning and civic life. Recreation centers might be abuzz with children's energy. Libraries can be filled with children reading, researching on the Internet, and doing their homework with adult mentors. Barbershops might be centers for discussing the issues of the day. The university might partner with local youth to create a community mural. A public forum involving local politicians, police, and residents might be taking place concerning neighborhood safety. In short, communities can be alive with civic learning.

The West Side of St. Paul in Minnesota is no different—with one important exception. Over the past ten years there has been an explicit effort to nurture the communities' potential to connect education in the community with civic life. This point can be illustrated in the story of two bus tours with two very different approaches to neighborhoods.

In 2004, community leaders brought a group of politicians on a bus tour to visit neighborhoods in the Twin Cities—but not just any neighborhoods. The bus took riders to drug-infested and high-crime areas where frightened parents told them about their fears and concerns for their children, who had to be instructed to avoid certain streets in the neighborhood. Residents talked about friends and neighbors who had been victims of crime. They talked about finding condom wrappers and dime bags in front of their houses and stores. The bus stopped at a local grocery store, where the owner explained that he was recently robbed at gunpoint—an all-to-common story. The purpose of the tour was, of course, to let politicians and policy makers see firsthand the difficulties in crime-ridden inner-city neighborhoods.[1]

This story, unfortunately, could have been about almost any inner-city neighborhood in the United States. Crime, violence, and fear are the prevalent perceptions of America's urban neighborhoods, where the focus is on the problems, deficits, and obstacles to individual success and community life. These stories are important and document the reality of too many Americans. But they also create a cultural narrative that guides the policy priorities and funding decisions made by well-intentioned politicians and policy experts who want to fix problems. The focus on deficits leads to the veritable industry of professional service providers and a massive criminal justice system, while undermining community-capacity-building initiatives that support civic learning.

This chapter tells a different story. On the West Side of St. Paul, young people from the neighborhood use a bus every weekday in the summer to attend formal and informal learning opportunities in their community. Several days after hearing the story of the Twin Cities bus tour on public radio I sat with a group of African American, Hmong, and Somali youths who were waiting for a bus at the West Side public library that would take them across the neighborhood to the Baker Recreational Center.

These youths were some of the 175 young people who use the "West Side Circulator" each day on the 7.5 mile loop that includes regular stops at learning sites and public places in the neighborhood, such as the Boys and Girls Club, Humboldt Junior and Senior High School, Our Lady of Guadalupe Church, and Torre de San Miguel housing. "The Circulator is a visible symbol that shows how where learning takes place is connected in a neighborhood," explains Nan Kari, one of the catalysts for the Neighborhood Learning Community, "and how learning happens in many places, not just the school."[2]

In this chapter, I examine the roots, approaches, and practices of the Neighborhood Learning Community, a contemporary community learning experiment, which, like Hull House and Highlander, deliberately ties education to civic life.

A Culture of Learning

The West Side Neighborhood Learning Community (NLC) is a network of people and organizations working collaboratively to strengthen learning in the West Side neighborhood of St. Paul. Since the mid-1990s, the group has been developing a neighborhood network that not only connects the multitude of learning opportunities available in the neighborhood, but also connects neighborhood-based learning with the creation of a vibrant civic life. Three ideas are central: recognizing the importance of place; seeing citizenship as active and co-creative; and engaging in public work that integrates civic practices into neighborhood life.[3]

In bringing these ideas to life, the network coordinates, catalyzes, and makes visible informal and formal learning. For the past decade, Neighborhood Learning Community organizers have provided leadership development, language learning, and intergenerational civic education in partnership with neighborhood residents. The NLC also aims to create meaningful learning partnerships across generations, ethnic groups, organizations, schools, and the neighborhood. Its participants bridge four generations. Between them, they speak more than five languages, and include long-time residents, new immigrants, college students, and young people One study found that 39 percent of those engaged in activities sponsored by the NLC are Hmong, 27 percent are white, 14 percent are Latino, 10 percent are Somali, and 10 percent belong to other ethnic groups.[4]

The organizations and people involved in the Neighborhood Learning Community work to create "a culture of learning" in the neighborhood: an environment for intergenerational learning that not only nurtures individual growth, but also develops an educative system on the neighborhood level in support of learning and civic life.[5] *A Community Alive with Learning*, a report based on the Neighborhood Learning Community, defines the goal as enabling children to grow up in a neighborhood:

> rich in learning opportunities, contexts and expectations. The neighborhood is a place dense with relationships, rich with history and memories, and alive with learning the skills, values, and aptitudes needed for an interdependent globalized world. Everyone is expected and invited to be a teacher, a learner and a co-creator of the common good.[6]

These neighborhood networks are pursued and reinforced through new ways of community practice that enable a growing number of people to contribute to the educational and civic life of the community. "We wanted to expand the opportunities for learning and create a tipping point that would transform the culture of the West Side," explains Nan Kari. The shift in culture, Kari says, is based on the "idea that learning for kids is supported if they live in a culture that is supportive of learning."[7]

Instead of viewing students as passive recipients of education, a culture of learning is centered in what NLC organizers term "co-creating learning opportunities."[8] And stories of co-creation are evident in the placed-based educational efforts of the West Side community.

Place-Based Education

As long ago as fall 1973, the West Side Citizens Organization (WSCO) formed as a permanent neighborhood organization after a series of political battles with the city to get a new school building for the West Side's only public high school, Humboldt High School. Its original aim of giving the West Side an organized voice in city affairs continues more than thirty years later, as does its commitment to community culture and history.[9]

"Democracy works only if citizens take the initiative to know one another and together plan the future," a 1973 editorial from the *West Side Voice*, the community newspaper, explains. Noting the grassroots efforts undertaken by West Side residents, it concludes, "Democracy gives us all responsibility."[10] As this editorial illustrates, community organizers on the West Side have a tradition of public work that includes looking at the strengths of the neighborhood to inspire democratic renewal.

For instance, one of the most popular sections of the *West Side Voice* in the 1970s and 1980s was a column entitled "West Side Story." This regular column detailed characters and stories from the old days of the West Side, a neighborhood that historically has been a hub for immigrants, starting with Jewish refuges from Russia and Eastern Europe in the late nineteenth century. Furthermore, in May 1983, convinced of the importance of community history, the West Side Citizens Organization (WSCO) convened a weekend conference on local history that included a tour of the area, a play, and an official designation of West Side History Days.

The importance of place on the West Side is also expressed through its public art, with more than sixty murals decorating street corners and buildings throughout the neighborhood. Caesar Chavez Avenue, one of its major streets, for instance, is filled with colorful murals, along with Latino stores and restaurants.

Murals focus on Latin American history, cultural symbols, and civil rights heroes such as Caesar Chavez, Mahatma Gandhi, and Martin Luther King Jr. "Historically, murals have been used by artists and communities to create a sense of identity, place, and culture," explains Aleida Benitez, a community organizer who coordinated several West Side murals led by neighborhood youths. "On the West Side, murals are a good way to bring youth and older residents together to communicate common ideas and dreams for the neighborhood." Noting that it is not only the process that matters, Benitez says, "The product is also important because it's a permanent reminder of the voice of the community."[11]

The murals are surrounded by other reminders of the strong local cultural identity in the neighborhood. On the busy corner of Caesar

Chavez Avenue and Congress St., El Burrito Mercado offers neighborhood residents the food, spices, music, fruits, and piñatas of their native Latin America. Since 1979, this family-owned business has done its best to replicate the community-building aspects of the mercados (marketplaces) of Mexico, providing a restaurant, deli, bakery, and meat department, along with produce and groceries.

The neighborhood is also filled with numerous Latino cultural groups. Since 1992, Theatro de Pueblo, a small Latin American theater group, has provided community theater and artistic educational programming. A Mexican Aztec dance group, Danza Mexica Cuauhtemoc, works to preserve the Mexica/Azteca culture by teaching ceremonies, warrior dances, and traditions, as well as the history, arts and craft, traditions, and language of Aztecs on the West Side. And the local settlement house, Neighborhood House, which was founded in 1897, organizes leadership and cultural groups for Hmong, Latino, African, and Russian immigrant adults and youths.

Sometimes called "the Ellis Island of the Midwest," the West Side continues to be a gateway for America's immigrant community. Nineteen percent of neighborhood residents were born outside the United States, and 35 percent of households speak a language other than English at home.

The Jewish immigrants from the turn of the twentieth century have been replaced by new Americans from Mexico, Southeast Asia, and East Africa. The racial/ethic demographics of the West Side have shifted drastically over the past two decades. The white population decreased from 66 percent to 49 percent between the 1990 and 2000 Census, while the Latino population grew from 21 percent to 33 percent over the same period. And growing populations of Southeast Asians and African immigrants continue to move into the neighborhood.

The public schools on the West Side are disproportionately attended by students from diverse backgrounds. Some 78 percent of students in West Side public schools are people of color.

Its diversity is not the only asset of the West Side. Another important asset is the neighborhood's unique geography. The 16,000 residents of the West Side's 4.6 square miles of land live in a uniquely located community, bounded on three sides by the Mississippi River, with the St. Paul city limits on the fourth. This geography makes creating a "neighborhood feeling" easier; it also renders the West Side an ideal place for neighborhood experimentation. The originators of the learning community concept realized this asset, noting that the geography on the West Side "creates a discrete neighborhood and clarity about place unlike many contiguous urban neighborhoods that are less well defined."[12]

Jane Addams School for Democracy

To understand the importance that place played in the creation of the Neighborhood Learning Community, it is important to understand the anchoring presence of the Jane Addams School. Beginning in 1996, students, staff, and faculty from the Center for Democracy and Citizenship at the Humphrey Institute, the University of Minnesota, and the College of St. Catherine met with staff from Neighborhood House to discuss the potential for a community-based democratic experiment on the West Side. These discussions led to the formation of the Jane Addams School for Democracy, named for Hull House's famous founder. An essential part of the mission, from the beginning, was to help reclaim the early settlement house tradition. Neighborhood House, which was founded at the turn of the twentieth century inspired by Jane Addams and other settlement pioneers, had few remaining elements from its early democratic roots, like so many other surviving settlement houses.

The Jane Addams School utilized not only the traditions of its namesake for inspiration, but also the model of education practiced by Myles Horton at Highlander Folk School. "We had knowledge of the traditions of Hull House and the Highlander Folk School and wanted to bring those ideas to life," explains John Wallace, a founder of the school. [13] Bringing the ideas to life in a modern context meant using some of the principles as guides, yet applying them to the particular desires of this unique neighborhood. Some principles were apparent from the earliest days. For instance, the founders saw the importance of a "learning circle" educational process where "everyone is a teacher and everyone is a learner." This was seen as both a model for democratic education and also an important means for overcoming power differentials that often exist in campus–community partnerships.

In addition, the partnership embodied the "public work" citizenship framework developed by Harry Boyte and the Center for Democracy and Citizenship at the University of Minnesota, along with Jane Addams School co-founders Nan Kari and Nan Skelton. With this approach, people from diverse backgrounds engage collaboratively in common work of public significance. [14]

The shape that the learning and collaborative action would take within these principles, however, would be ever-changing and determined by those who came to participate. Such flexibility is reminiscent of the founding of social settlement houses at the end of the nineteenth century. Canon Barnett, founder of the original settlement house in London, once described the distinguishing feature of Toynbee Hall and the settlement movement as "the absence of program and the presence of men and women who recognize the obligations of citizenship."[15] It is this spirit of co-creation that the Jane Addams School attempts to recapture.

Nan Skelton describes its founding in language similar to the founding stories of Addams's Hull House and Horton's Highlander:

> We got to the end of a summer of conversations [in 1996] and we didn't have a set plan. But it didn't seem appropriate to say, "Okay, here are the structures, here are the lesson plans, and here are the rules." We thought we should get started and let people teach us what it is they want to learn. We'd then figure out what we needed to learn to address those issues.[16]

With the hope of "letting people teach each other what they wanted to learn" the Jane Addams School was launched on September 23, 1996, with "reciprocity as the guiding feature." The first night on the second floor of Neighborhood House, thirty people speaking three different languages showed up, including some children. There were no interpreters and no child care. And yet the organizers had faith in the power of people to take initiative, be creative, and learn together. "At Jane Addams School what we've done is what Myles Horton advises: we've put people together in the same room and not let it get more complicated than that," Wallace says. He then explains simply, "We trust the process."[17]

The first night of the learning exchange was memorable, and might have shaken the trust of the most faithful community practitioner. John Wallace began by explaining, "None of us are expert teachers, so we're all going to have to become experts in learning." It was an echo of Bernice Robinson, first teacher of the Citizenship Schools during the civil rights movement. The learning interest of the community residents was not what the visitors from the university had hoped for—or even an issue they felt qualified to address. "It became pretty clear that what people wanted was to pass the citizenship exam," recalls Skelton, who then asked herself: "Couldn't there be something else?"[18]

And yet the group persisted. By the end of that first evening three things were achieved: participants could say "My name is . . ." in Hmong, English, and Spanish; Hmong and Spanish-speaking immigrants learned to say and read "cit," the first syllable of the word "citizen"; and the group left undiscouraged, and filled with a sense of possibility.[19]

The impressive results of the now more than ten years of the Jane Addams School have been well documented and include more than 1,000 immigrants passing the citizenship exam; youths organizing local, national, and international public work projects; and intergenerational dialogues, community festivals, and public art projects.[20] Today, hundreds of people meet two nights a week at Humboldt High School in "learning circles" partnering new immigrants with American-born English speakers. The circles include two "Hmong circles," one "Spanish circle," one "East African circle," one "organizing circle," one "homework group" for youth, and several "children's circles."

Projects over the past years include citizenship-test preparation, language exchange, and homework help, as well as organizing to improve the U.S. citizenship exam, reform the local schools, and increase the pressure on the U.S. government to bring fundamental human rights to Laos. Terri Wilson, who first came to the Jane Addams School as an undergraduate student, pointed to the holistic approach of the school when she explains how it "gave me the space and responsibility to do things I never thought I could do, like be a leader and facilitator, and share laughter with a 74 year old woman across language and culture." She continues, "The space of Jane Addams School is a space where my contributions are seen as valuable; a space that recognizes rather than overlooks people's diverse talents and creativity." Now as a graduate student studying education reform and still involved with the Jane Addams School, Wilson reflects, "I've learned, above all else, that asking questions implies a commitment to respond."[21]

Civic leadership development is also a component of the learning circles. Participants gain skills in leadership, facilitation, public speaking, and cross-cultural competency. While most immigrants come to the Jane Addams School simply to pass the U.S. citizenship exam and practice speaking English, many find that in the process they gain civic capacities and a civic identity. Koua Yang Her, a Hmong immigrant involved from the early days of the school, explains, "Jane Addams School has taught me that I have the power to help my community. There is a power when people share ideas and work together. One thing is for sure: one person can't do it alone."[22]

Founding the Neighborhood Learning Community

With an awareness that one person—or organization—can't do it alone, in 2001, an "Education Dialogue" was convened by the Jane Addams School and the West Side Citizens Organization (WSCO), building on community dialogues launched by the West Side Family Center a few years earlier. At that forum, fifty people who lived or worked in the community gathered to share their concerns about education, and to discuss the formal and informal learning opportunities that existed on the West Side. Out of this process, and a series of conversations that followed, the

Neighborhood Learning Community (NLC) was created as a network for learning. It soon obtained funds to support its efforts from local and national foundations, including a four-year Wallace Foundation grant.

In many ways, the NLC also formed as a response to the expanding role that leaders involved with the Jane Addams School began to play in the West Side neighborhood, or, as some of the founders describe it, because these grassroots educational efforts started to "leak out" into the broader neighborhood. For instance, college students involved with the Jane Addams School started a local gardening project. Eventually, the project enabled young people to garden each week at a nearby community-supported agriculture (CSA) farm and bring fresh farm produce to the food shelf at Neighborhood House. This led Gunnar Liden, a college student involved with the Jane Addams School, to create the Youth Farm and Market Project on the West Side. Today Liden is the executive director of Youth Farm, and Mary Lee Vang, who became involved with the Jane Addams School as a youth, is the West Side Youth Farm Coordinator.

At the same time, Jane Addams School leaders worked with St. Paul Community Education to diversify their classes by having immigrants involved with the Jane Addams School teach cultural classes in cooking, sewing, and dancing; an Americorp member, D'Ann Lesch, who has since worked as an organizer on the West Side, started Public Achievement, the Center for Democracy and Citizenship's youth civic engagement initiative, at the West Side's Humboldt High School; and partnerships were developing with a diverse group of West Side organizations, from the community development corporation to the local citizen's association.

The NLC started with a core group of community organizations, with somewhat less ownership by residents of the local neighborhood. As in the early days of Hull House, NLC leaders found it necessary to find ways to give more ownership directly to community residents. Thus, mini-grants were offered to learning-centered projects led by youth and community residents for community initiatives, and parents and community organizations for school initiatives. Among the recipients were elementary school students who developed a historic tour of the West Side through oral histories, a local artist who created a photographic essay documenting the diversity of the West Side for display at the neighborhood market, a local dance group that teaches young people about Aztec language, dance, song, and customs, and the local community development corporation, which offers courses for young people on micro-credit lending. Grant reviewers were composed solely of community residents (including youth), giving power—through funding and decision-making authority—directly to the neighborhood.

The learning network expanded, developing partnerships with additional community residents and community institutions (businesses, schools, and nonprofits). Based on these experiences, Nan Skelton notes that the partnerships in this learning community have not been static: "It's like when you create a pathway: if you create it and never walk on it, the pathway becomes overgrown. It goes away. But if you keep walking it, the pathway gets stronger and stronger."

Skelton, who was crucial to the development of the Neighborhood Learning Community, reflects that she is beginning to see an impact from these partnerships. "You've got to traverse [the pathway] all the time. But that's starting to happen. People are starting to believe that maybe there is something going on here that is worth keeping going and doing more of."[23]

Partner Organizations

The ecology of civic learning is given meaning by the efforts to create these "pathways" connecting the institutions on the West Side where learning is taking place—especially in the many partner organizations working collaboratively to create a learning network that connects education with civic life.

Each of the organizations involved with the NLC has a formal or informal educational component, though they do not always describe their work in this way. The NLC becomes a connector that links these organizations as a network. As Kari Denissen, the first NLC staff member, explains, "A strong value is placed on doing relational work. The belief was that in order for kids to do well there needs to be an infrastructure, a web of organizations, and there needs to be a way for them to work together in a healthy partnership way that isn't forced; and [also] isn't, 'I'll collaborate with you because we have to write this grant.' [Rather], it's about authentic relationships."[24]

The web of organizations has several tiers of involvement. Organizations represented on a "coordinating council" of the NLC provide leadership. The founding organizations are mainstays on this group, and include the Jane Addams School, the West Side Citizens Organization (WSCO), the Center for Democracy and Citizenship at the Humphrey Institute, Youth Farm and Market Project, El Rio Vista Recreation Center, St. Paul Community Education, and Danza Mexica Cuahetemoc (an Aztec dance group).

Other organizations play a leadership role on various aspects of the network, including the Riverview Library, Neighborhood House, Humboldt Senior High School, Baker Recreation Center, Urban 4-H, Girl Scout Council of St. Croix Valley, the West Side Family Center, and the

Minnesota Department of Agriculture. Finally, many organizations support some aspects of the learning activities of the NLC, including community organizations (e.g., the Boys and Girls Club), the local schools (e.g., Riverview Elementary, Roosevelt Elementary, Cherokee Elementary, Humboldt Junior High School, and St. Matthew's Elementary), local churches (e.g., Cherokee Methodist Church and La Puerta Abierta), local businesses (e.g., Jerebeks Coffee House), local community development corporations (e.g., Riverview Economic Development Association and Neighborhood Development Association), and local arts organizations (e.g., Theatro del Pueblo).

Turning Traffic Flow Around

The focus on partnering in support of learning represents an important conceptual shift. Many community initiatives follow Dewey's original conception of the "school as a social center," with parents, social workers, community organizations, and other institutions orbiting around the school. With this in mind, Elona Street Stewart, the chair of the St. Paul school board, concludes that schools need to "shift the power and the control."[25]

"We need to listen to street corner conversations and turn traffic flow around," Stewart explained. "Instead of community coming into schools, [we need schooling to] go out to the community." She suggested, for example, having teachers, school board members, and administrators serve on community boards and become active in the broader community. This type of community engagement would set an example, she argued, because "school people need to know whose front porch is most important on the block."[26]

Echoing Dewey, Jerome Stein terms this shift in perspective a "Copernican Revolution" in education, adding, "When we finally acknowledge that schools orbit communities and families, things will get a lot simpler."[27] The idea of making parents and community central is supported by a series of research studies on effective student learning. Henderson and Mapp, for example, found that students do better when parents, community groups, and schools work in collaboration, rather than in isolation.[28] Laurence Steinberg's study of schools in *Beyond the Classroom* supports these findings.

Steinberg and his research team studied student achievement based on what took place in homes, peer groups, and communities, rather than in schools. Steinberg found that while schools are an important influence on student achievement, school time is only one of many influences—and not even the most important one. The failure of school reform, he concludes, is its overemphasis on the school; to be successful, education reform must also emphasize the places that have the most impact on student learning—areas beyond the classroom. He finds: "No curricular overhaul, no instructional innovation, no toughening of standards, no rethinking of teacher training or compensation will succeed if students do not come to schools interested in, and committed to, learning."[29]

The impact that parental involvement has on school performance and student achievement also has been well documented.[30] For educators struggling inside the classroom, the importance of parental involvement cannot be overstated. And yet most efforts to include parents emphasize participating in the schools as they exist, with a "school-centric" focus.[31] This model "assumes an uncritical stance of parents toward the dominant culture of the school."[32]

However, in examining the role that parents play in the Texas Industrial Areas Foundation (IAF), a chapter of the community organizing group founded by Saul Alinsky, Dennis Shirley finds a "new kind of parental engagement." This model emphasizes parents as active citizens working to "transform schools and the neighborhood."[33] Moreover, this new kind of engagement "transcends accommodationist approaches to school and community relationships by bringing the community into the heart of the school and using the school as a base for the political revitalization of the community."[34]

"Learning takes buy-in from parents. [You] need parents to want kids to look at the neighborhood as a place of learning," a West Side teacher observed approvingly of the efforts to create a culture of learning. He continued, "You need to get parents involved first; then it's easier to get kids involved."[35] Parental involvement, within a culture of learning, means not only inviting community into the school, but also inviting schooling into the community. This occurs when communities support children's learning, and when community residents are encouraged to follow their own learning aspirations. This approach was used for the Labor Museum at Hull House and for the Citizenship Schools at Highlander, and it is central in creating a culture of learning on the West Side.

School-centered approaches, however, have dominated educational reform movements for the past century.[36] Developing a neighborhood culture of learning counters these prevailing trends and invites non-experts to participate in educational reform. This holistic view is consistent with a citizen-centered model for public action that asks experts to hold back their professional diagnosis and frameworks—to simply be "on tap," rather than "on top."[37] This involves several paradigm shifts: seeing ordinary people as producers, not consumers; actors, not spectators, and teachers, not students (see Figure 5.1).

Table 5.1   Traditional Learning versus Culture of Learning

TRADITIONAL LEARNING	CULTURE OF LEARNING
School-centered	Education in the Community
Expert-centered	Citizen-centered
Youth-centered	Intergenerational
Linear	Systemic
Experts on top	Experts on tap
Consumers	Producers
Spectators	Actors
Students	Teachers and Learners

Community Initiatives and Public Practices

When these ideas frame an educational initiative, it represents a conceptual shift that undergirds programming, as evidenced by the community initiatives and public practices described next. This approach runs contrary to many of the dominant views of citizen/learners in public life.

Creating an orbit where the schools participate in, contribute to, and support community learning is essential to the efforts of the Neighborhood Learning Community. Parents and community residents are both primary vehicles for civic learning as well as supporters of school-based learning. The community initiatives and public practices are attempting to "turn traffic flow around" by reworking neighborhood transportation, making visible formal and informal learning opportunities, bridging programs of the West Side's youth-serving organizations, and creating multiple opportunities for public art and community celebrations.

West Side Circulator: Reworking Neighborhood Transportation and Relationships

In 2003, through the joint efforts of parents and seventeen West Side youth-serving organizations, the West Side Circulator began providing free bus service to learning sites and public places in the neighborhood. More than 6,300 riders used the Circulator in that first summer and it continues to be both an important resource for the West Side and a model for the rest of the city.

The Circulator, for instance, increases participation in neighborhood programs in the summer months and allows youth to participate in a more diverse range of activities. "So many kids ask about the Circulator that we had to put the schedule on the door," explains Mary Margaret Sullivan, the librarian on the West Side branch of the public library. Sullivan added, "Many kids who would not normally come to the library come because of the Circulator," which is especially important for a public library struggling to maintain its relevancy in an age when access to information is no longer centralized. In many ways, the Circulator, which increased library usage, is helping the library once again to be considered a "people's university," serving the public through collaboration and networking.[38]

As one might expect, some West Side organizations were reluctant to combine resources to provide a central mode of transportation, guided by the instincts that have become necessary for survival in the competitive funding world of nonprofits. Within this atmosphere, organizations are forced to cover their own programs first, rather than collaborate.

However, the early success of the Circulator made it easier for organizations to see the benefits of collaboration. "[The Circulator has] been latched onto by the other organizations that used to set aside money for vans and transportation," explains the former WSCO board chair, Bob Cudahy. Cudahy, who is also a teacher, added, "The Circulator is the kind of thing that might not show up on people's radar in terms of learning because it's not formal learning. But it makes educational opportunities possible. It's important to get kids to programs, keeping them thinking, and helping them become lifelong learners."[39]

All-Around-the-Neighborhood Summer Camps: A New Way of Working Together

In communities, successful collaboration often leads to more collaboration. Many of the West Side community organizers credit the NLC with developing "a new way of working together" among organizations on the West Side. The success of the Circulator resulted in conversations among parents and youth-serving organizations about how best to provide learning opportunities for children in the neighborhood leading to All-Around-the-Neighborhood, which began as a nine-week summer camp in 2004 and expanded to year-round programs both inside and out-of-school in 2005. The NLC touts All-Around the Neighborhood as "a learning program that invites children ages six to twelve, older youth, and adults to explore the entire West Side neighborhood as a living classroom."

This collaborative approach allows organizations to focus on strengths to provide a diverse (and fun) set of summer programs for neighborhood youths—and the Circulator provides transportation. The program includes weekly themes, with cohorts studying different issues each week, such as cultural cuisine and nutrition, sports and health, visual arts, theater and performance, community leadership, environmental stewardship, and ancient sciences. Each week a new West Side organization coordinates the programming.

One of the community teachers talks about the importance of place in this learning experiment: "We spent about thirty minutes every day walking through the neighborhood." Describing everyday experiences that are part of the life of the neighborhood, like meeting people working on their houses and in their gardens, the educator concluded, "I think the experience of connecting with people made the community real to them."[40] One of the teachers who lives in the neighborhood reported, "It really does build a sense of community."[41]

Celebrating Community and Public Work

The neighborhood celebrates the diverse cultures on the West Side with an annual Freedom Festival. Each summer since 1998, hundreds of neighborhood residents from different cultural backgrounds and from all ages come together to celebrate their visions for democracy originally at Parque Castillo, and more recently at La Puerta Abierta Church, which is also the site of Youth Farm's community gardens.

Activities include a set of performances and recognitions for the year's work. Along with children playing games, the festival is filled with Asian, Mexican, and African home-cooked cuisine. Hmong immigrants perform traditional dances. There is a fashion show with beautiful traditional clothing from countries such as Peru, Mexico, India, and Laos. Politicians, such as the late Senator Paul Wellstone and late Representative Bruce Vento, along with state Senator Mee Moua, the first Hmong-elected state official in the nation, give short speeches to honor new American citizens for passing the citizenship test that year. In the summer of 2006, the festival honored 74 new U.S. citizens. These new citizens also tell stories of their journeys from foreign countries, such as Somalia, Mexico, and Laos. These activities, when put together, illustrate an important set of public practices that have been developed over the past few years.

Many policy makers and scholars express concern over declining political participation.[42] This phenomenon, at least partially, is attributed to the lack of recognition and immediate satisfaction from participation in the slow, compromise-ridden world of conventional politics. The public practices of the Freedom Festival offer guidance for how politics can become more grounded in a relational, yet diverse, public community.

People who participated in political actions are recognized with public acknowledgments within the context of a community. Organizers of the event call people to the stage who wrote letters to politicians, lobbied the state legislature, or participated in various organizing projects at the Jane Addams School. Immigrants and college students (two politically disenfranchised groups) are always celebrated with encouraging words, flowers, and public recognition. Aleida Benitez, who helped organize the first Freedom Festival and was herself honored as a new citizen at the 2004 festival, observes, "The Freedom Festival celebrates community accomplishments." Benitez adds, "It unites the community and also celebrates diverse cultures through crafts, dance, music, [and a] fashion show. It's a way of honoring everyday heroes: elders, young people, and immigrants."[43] This celebration of community and public work also represents a different kind of politics.

The festival planning process is an opportunity for young people to learn the skills and practice of this different kind of politics. For example, Chao Moua, one youth who helped plan the festival as part of the Youth Apprenticeship Project, explains some of the things he learned from playing a leadership role in the community festival:

> When I first started at Jane Addams School I was really shy. Now I see how things get planned. And I know I have the power to do what I want. I've learned that it's not easy to plan a community festival. When you just go to them you don't see it. But when you plan it, you have to figure out things like who to invite for speakers, how to get people to come, and how to organize the fashion show. . . . I got to do public speaking at the Freedom Festival, and I feel more comfortable talking in front of others now.[44]

Youth Apprenticeship Project: Making Civic Contributions

Each week a group of West Side youths meet as part of an urban 4–H group at the West Side public housing complex. The group helps to design and lead daylong out-of-school learning opportunities for younger children. In the process they learn public speaking, curriculum design, and group facilitation skills. When adults in the neighborhood asked the group what they really wanted, they said paid jobs to do the kinds of things they did as part of their neighborhood youth group. With this suggestion, the idea for the Youth Apprenticeship Project was born.[45]

Within the broader context of the NLC, the Youth Apprenticeship Project provides summer employment in West Side nonprofits for high school students who live or go to school on the West Side. Each summer, approximately twenty-five teens spend ten weeks working with a mentor at a West Side organization or business. They also work on other aspects of the NLC, like planning the Freedom Festival or working with All-Around-the Neighborhood.

Teenagers choose to work with organizations throughout the West Side that take a variety of approaches to making an impact in the community. They apprentice at direct service organizations, such as the neighborhood food shelf, youth development organizations, such as parks and recreation centers, community organizing projects, such as those at the local community council, and electoral initiatives, such as a West Side effort to register eligible residents. They also serve as lead organizers doing community gardening, along with other projects, such as cooking, photography, and community youth leadership, at Youth Farm and Market Project.

A set of "coaches" from the neighborhood helps lead reflection sessions each week. The diverse sets of experiences center upon a unifying theme. For example, past themes have included "Human Rights on the West Side and the World" and "Race, Culture, and Identity," each of which was woven into the weekly reflection sessions on the young people's community work. Youths also conduct oral histories with family members and other West Side residents to capture some of the stories and cultures from the neighborhood.

These apprenticeships make a point of reflecting on the public dimensions of their host organizations and the civic dimensions of their work. Giving young people experience with personally fulfilling work that makes a meaningful public contribution is a deliberate aim of the apprenticeship. "We think that there aren't a lot of places where kids can learn that they can make civic contributions through work," explains Nan Kari, who helped develop the curriculum. "We wanted to find a way to weave together work and citizenship."[46]

As with the efforts of the broader Neighborhood Learning Community, youth work collaboratively in their efforts and sometimes help local organizations collaborate in ways that may not otherwise have occurred. For example, a youth assigned to organize neighborhood block parties partnered with a youth working on voter registration by making voter registration materials and resources available at each of the thirty-eight summer block parties that were organized—a powerful youth-led example of connecting education in the community with civic engagement.

Other youths worked to combat violence on the West Side by offering intergenerational dialogues, social events, and community dances. They publicized learning opportunities on the West Side in a directory that will also be an interactive Web site, so, as one youth explained, "people can be more informed about what their neighborhood is into." The directory will include information on neighborhood organizations, stores, businesses, popular places, and public art.

Still others collected and documented the oral histories of Hmong elders to learn more about and honor their cultural traditions. In describing the diversity of options for community engagement as part of the apprenticeship, Kari Denissen explains, "We want them to think about making change in a community and see that there are a lot of ways to make change."[47]

Finally, one youth worked with a neighborhood lawyer and WSCO to examine restorative justice and community circles. The youth interviewed a diverse group of stakeholders with an interest in criminal justice. "I learned that restorative justice is a way to make communities whole—it's about restoring communities when things have gone wrong." The youth also began to think about the potential benefit this community-based approach could bring not only to communities, but also to the disciplinary policies of schools.[48]

In focus groups with young people involved with the Youth Apprentice Project, several themes emerged, including the importance of productive work and the significance of getting to know the neighborhood.[49]

Doing Productive Work

Creating space for young people to share their voices on public issues and engage in community-problem solving are important elements of the Youth Apprenticeship Project, as articulated by the youth who participate. They learned to play a leadership role on community projects and "take charge of a group," as one reported.

This also meant moving beyond the roles of participants or service providers. "I've done more community projects, and learned how to put on projects and lead different groups in the community." Another youth commented on the community organizing skills he was developing, "I have to talk with lead organizers of different companies, people [teens] wouldn't normally talk to. At first it was intimidating, we were calling businesses around the West Side and just trying to talk with these people and they didn't know who we were. But then you establish connections with people."

One youth talked about the role of youth in reducing neighborhood violence. "[Having youth more involved in decision-making is] what we're working toward. I met my boss at a meeting about gangs with the police and there were [only] like five youth there. They wouldn't let me talk and I was like, 'Wait. Hold on. I should know more about gangs than you. We're younger. We're going through it.'"

Youth leadership encouraged a more youth-friendly response. Based on this initial meeting, several youth worked to organize a community dialogue with young people talking with adults about the issues of gangs and crime. The dialogue enabled youths to talk with their peers and then with adults about violence. "When we were talking about follow-up, all the adults were like 'let's have another dialogue' and the teens were like, 'No, that sounds really boring. Let's have a community dance.'" This led to a community-wide dance organized by several youth apprentices called "Mix it Up."

Based on her experiences, one youth advised: "If something is not going well in the neighborhood, get a group together, talk about it, and help out to make change. . . . We try to help out to solve the problem. We're trying to make the grown-ups listen to us."

Getting to Know the Local Neighborhood

Another important aspect of the Youth Apprenticeship Project is getting to know about the local community, including its characteristics, history, and resources. One youth commented, "Before I started doing this, I never knew about all these organizations and I've been living here for twelve years." Another observed: "There are a lot of learning opportunities, if you look for them. A lot of people don't know about them. We're trying to make that change, but it's only the beginning. This is a good place to live if you know what you have here."

"It helps seeing all the people come together. It shows how important it is to get to know your neighborhood," explained one youth. He noted the importance of the garden, which provides "a really good way to get people to come together." In discussing the market, one youth noted how public performances helped attract customers, "We used to set up a little tent. Now people come to see the performances and the dancers."

In everyday neighborhood life, one youth said that it's difficult to "see the community as a whole," noting that Cherokee Heights Elementary School can seem like a different world from where he lived on the other side of the neighborhood. And yet, the youth observed that when Youth Farm has the markets, "It brings different parts of the neighborhood together."

Obstacles: The School/Community Divide

Bringing different parts of the neighborhood together, however, is not enough. In the midst of an interview with Elona Street Stewart, the first Native American elected to a school board in an urban district in Minnesota, I was pressing for other partnering opportunities where schools and communities might work together, when she stopped me and pointedly asked, "Are the schools ready for a group of competent, engaged people saying, 'We're here'?"[50] This important community advocate obviously had doubts.

This challenge is symptomatic of obstacles that face the Neighborhood Learning Community in its efforts to improve education. It highlights the very different cultures that are not only endemic in schools, but also in community-based organizations. Recognizing and overcoming these obstacles are essential for successfully educating democratic citizens.

It often seems as though a giant wall exists between schools and communities, a wall reinforced by people on both sides of the divide. A school board member recognizes that "when people in the community talk, 'we' does not include schools at all in meaningful community conversations." She warns, "That needs to change."[51]

Community educators are also aware of this divide. One organizer laments, "A lot of times teachers and school staff feel like they have to be on the defensive because community is coming to critique schools or tell teachers what they're doing wrong. There's a sense that when a community person comes, [school officials think] what do you really want?" The organizer adds, "There's a lot of distrust."

Specialized Ways of Knowing

The barriers put in place by an overly professional approach to education, with emphasis on specialized and credentialized ways of knowing, are an obstacle that widens this divide and makes neighborhoods becoming places of civic learning more difficult. The messiness of informal education is given little value in this paradigmatic stance. Harry Boyte describes the professionalizing impulse in which "conventional experts imagine their specialized knowledge to be the superior (or even singular or sufficient) resource in solving problems."[52] In the field of education, this is actualized through an emphasis on credentials, techniques, specialization, and finding the "one best way" to achieve fixed ends.

The expert model also leads to fragmentation; the community is not seen as a legitimate site for learning, nor are people outside the school viewed as co-educators. When the school does interact with the broader community, it often involves one-directional service delivery. For instance, in community service projects that are organized by schools, the stance is often that of the "outside expert," with schools providing service to "needy" recipients.[53] Even when reflection is included in course-based community service, the community is most often seen as the site for making a difference, while the classroom is regarded as the place to reflect on and learn from community experiences.

The inability to see the many resources in the community is illustrated in the most common ways that schools invite community participation—namely, through tutoring. Noting the lack of imagination in viewing communities as co-educators, one West Side organizer laments, "The community has an important role [in formal schooling], but it's not an educational role. And even when it's an educational role, then it's [the community members being asked to provide] tutoring assistance or helping with formal education."[54]

Narrow Curriculum and the Need for Quantifiable Results

Communities often have difficulty interesting teachers in incorporating a civic leadership component into the curriculum, especially given the pressures that come from the increasing mandates of high-stakes testing. In most schools, the existing burdens on underresourced teachers make the idea of community learning seem unrealistic. And even when teachers are interested, logistical concerns such as students' schedules or transportation issues make it challenging for teams to work consistently in the community for longer periods of time.

The reality is that many teachers themselves are unfamiliar with public and community issues in the local neighborhood, especially in inner-city neighborhoods, and do not feel confident in assuming the role of civic educators promoting community engagement.

Moreover, there is the related issue of evaluation and measurement of impact. Schools, government agencies and, increasingly, foundations tend to emphasize quantifiable outcomes, rather than meaningful civic learning. However, it is difficult to determine causal relationships between learning through community engagement and conventional school-based measures.

With little success in evaluating impact, community initiatives often resort to counting bodies as their best measure of success. "We learned when organizations that are organized around service delivery think about their work with kids, they think about how many kids came. They ask: 'What's the activity?' rather than 'What's the learning?'" explains Nan Kari.[55] It is almost impossible to keep track of the many outcomes that occur in a neighborhood trying to create "an abundance of learning." More often, community practice is captured in stories and qualitative research—as in this study. Making these findings visible, relevant, and practical is an obstacle for school-community partnerships.

Promising Practices

A recent report on the Neighborhood Learning Community concludes that strong schools need strong communities, and strong communities can build strong schools.[56] For this to occur, it requires using informal, as well as formal education; connecting the many places where education for democracy takes place; and deliberately linking education in the community with civic education. At least three practices developed as part of the NLC hold promise for other communities interested in broadening its educational resources.

A Community Connector

The NLC network plays the essential role in "bringing different parts of the neighborhood together." The network acts as a "mediating institution," connecting education taking place in the community with participants and civic life. A significant part of the mediation work between the schools and the community is done by a full-time staff member for the NLC. The position was named after the essential role played by "community connectors" in making change in Malcolm Gladwell's *The Tipping Point*.[57]

The Community Connector position is designed to "help build relationships and keep an eye on the whole map and makes connections where it makes sense to make connections." Kari Denissen, who served as Community Connector from 2002–2005 and continues to provide leadership, explains: "Sometimes [partnerships] come out of sustained relationships where I just hang out at organizations because a lot of it is about trust. Why should someone trust me if I show up and say: 'You should do this,' as opposed to being there for four months and seeing what they do?"[58]

A partner involved with the NLC explains why the mediating role of this network is so important: "You can have the community involved in an issue, but when there is too much [of a complicated] institutional process, people tend to disengage." Mediating institutions, such as the Neighborhood Learning Community, can play a role in catalyzing engagement by giving people concrete ways to participate strategically so they didn't feel overwhelmed and powerless to affect change. In the search for a new principal at Humboldt High School, for example, the NLC organized several community forums with potential candidates and developed a process for meaningful community input.[59]

Thus, the NLC network coordinates relationships between community institutions and helps neighborhood residents connect with larger, impersonal institutions—such as schools, local government, state elected officials, and the Immigration and Naturalization Service—that impact people's daily lives.

Youth Empowerment through Public Achievement

A second promising practice is generated by youth empowerment. Since 1997, for example, the Center for Democracy and Citizenship, led by D'Ann Lesch, an organizer for the center, has partnered with Humboldt High School and Junior ROTC to offer high school students the opportunity to participate in Public Achievement, an international youth civic engagement initiative. In Public Achievement, young people work with adult coaches to implement public work projects on issues of their choosing. Through this process, Humboldt students have tackled school-based issues, such as the need for cleaner bathrooms; community issues, such as neighborhood safety; national issues, such as racism and sexism; and international issues, such as improving human rights in Laos.

Public Achievement, which started in Minnesota in the early 1990s, directly incorporates the lessons of the Citizenship Schools of the Highlander Folk School. Harry Boyte, who is one of the founders of Public Achievement, also worked as a young man with the Citizenship Schools as an organizer for the Southern Christian Leadership Conference (SCLC) in the 1960s. The Citizenship Schools help inform "the framing of Public Achievement as about both developing active citizenship essential for a flourishing democracy and challenging the inadequacy of conventional meanings of political concepts such as citizenship, politics, and democracy itself," writes Boyte.[60]

I was among the adult coaches who worked with the Citizenship Group, a five-year project that was an outgrowth of Public Achievement on the West Side. The group of high school students who attended Humboldt High School and participated in the Jane Addams School worked to improve the way the United States measures citizenship. Composed mostly of immigrant youth, the group researched the history of the U.S. citizenship exam, making several visits to the Immigration and Naturalization Service's regional offices. They then created a video illustrating the difficulty U.S. citizens have with questions on the exam (such as "What were the original 13 colonies?" and "How many amendments are there to the Constitution?").

Of the twenty-five people the group interviewed on tape, only one U.S. citizen answered three out of five questions correctly. American citizens, for example, thought Minnesota and California were among the original thirteen colonies, that Roosevelt was the first commander-in-chief of the U.S. military, and that there are thousands of amendments to the U.S. Constitution. Having fun with the lack of knowledge of basic civics by U.S. citizens, the video made the point that citizenship is a contested idea and the ideals of citizenship need to include active participation, along with civic knowledge.

The group presented these findings locally and nationally at conferences and meetings; they raised more than $7,000 to travel to Washington, D.C., to discuss the issue with their congressional representatives, including the late Senator Paul Wellstone, Senator Mark Dayton, and Representative Betty McCollum; and received local press and other recognition for their efforts.[61]

Ultimately, a national commission was formed to study the issue and a new exam is being piloted. A St. Paul *Pioneer Press* article captured the importance of these kinds of grassroots organizing efforts to help bring national attention to the need for reforming the citizenship exam: "It's true that the Humboldt students didn't force the issue onto the national agenda," Webb reported. "Rather, they were part of a grassroots movement that saw a problem where others did not, pushed for reform and helped raise the issue to greater prominence."[62]

The success of the Citizenship Group illustrates the potential impact of the ecology of civic learning. The group partnered with a number of institutions—including Public Achievement (the initial home for the group), the Jane Addams School (which provided support from Hmong elders and college students), Metropolitan State University (which offered funding and two-semesters of academic credit for the group to work on the issue), Equity Trust (a community loan fund that provided funding), and the St. Paul *Pioneer Press* (that chronicled their efforts in a series of articles)—in their efforts to make a sustained commitment to change. This illustrates the larger lesson that while Humboldt High School helped catalyze the Citizenship Group through Public Achievement, it takes a broader community-based civic infrastructure to keep the momentum going.

Educator Training Through the West Side Teachers Institute

In a third promising practice for effective school–community partnerships, the Neighborhood Learning Community focuses on the training of educators. The NLC found that an important area for leveraging the integration of community learning with the classroom is through teacher preparation. With some initial success, as well as some recruiting setbacks, the NLC has partnered with the local public schools through the Teachers Institute, a credit-bearing class for St. Paul educators to connect their curriculum with community engagement.

In its first two years, the project involved several St. Paul schoolteachers studying the benefits of and obstacles to community engagement, along with practical course-planning with a community component. One of the teachers involved with the institute explains, "It's a good way to get teachers thinking about how to get kids involved in community."[63] Teachers appreciated the chance to really talk with other teachers. These substantive conversations on the art of teaching, as Deborah Meier notes, are all too uncommon between adults in schools.[64] To this end, teachers appreciated that the class was "done in a circle," centered on "stories based on personal experiences," and that there was a "chance to collaborate with other teachers."[65]

To further develop the concept of community as co-educator, the third year of the Teachers Institute involved an equal number of organizers from local nonprofits and public school teachers as students in the institute, each with the option of receiving graduate credit. The reworked institute shifted its focus to a more team-oriented learning approach. "We found that when teachers were working on individual community projects, they did not work as a team," explains Nan Kari, one of the leaders of the Institute. "Now we ask, 'What kind of vision do we want to work for?' and all projects work toward that goal."[66]

In the early sessions, the group created a collective vision for the West Side community: "People of all ages are supported by formal and informal learning experiences where everyone is a teacher, a learner, and member of the community." With this shared vision, participants mapped out projects collaboratively. For instance, one project linked Youth Apprenticeship Project with Humboldt High School to enable youth to get high school credit, along with a year-round community engagement experience. This provides another example of the relational and comprehensive dimensions of the NLC, and how, over time, community-based efforts reach *into* the schools.

More than One Neighborhood: Minnesota Working Together

The Neighborhood Learning Community concept of connecting democratic community education with public work that began more than ten years ago with the creation of the Jane Addams School has many important lessons to teach us about creating a culture of civic learning in a contemporary setting. This work builds on the efforts of Hull House and the Highlander Folk School, and illustrates that these historical traditions have great relevancy to the struggles to revitalize education, community, and democracy in the twenty-first century.

An important lesson that has emerged as the group has attempted to sustain its efforts in an atmosphere that relies on grant-funding is that one neighborhood can't do it alone. While innovation might start with a couple of individuals working collaboratively in a "different way," over time neighborhood-based efforts also need to influence systems to sustain creativity. Thus, this initiative, which began with a few dozen people trying to create something unique in a single neighborhood, is now attempting to bring about larger structural change. The leaders involved in the NLC have begun to expand their efforts to influence city and state systems in a variety of ways so other neighborhoods can connect education to civic life.

Using the Neighborhood Learning Community as a model, for example, Chris Coleman, St. Paul's new mayor, is putting an emphasis on what he calls "the second shift," learning after the schoolday, to ensure that all children get what they need to succeed. On the state level, the Center for Democracy and Citizenship has launched Minnesota Works Together to improve the civic life and values of Minnesota. This initiative, using the NLC as its flagship, is attempting to "show Minnesota as a civic laboratory for the nation," says Harry Boyte, who is spearheading the project. With funding from the Kellogg Foundation, Minnesota Works Together is examining the connections between public policy and civic life and launching a statewide conversation to put citizens at the center of politics. Using the lesson from the NLC that culture change is possible, this important initiative hopes to help reclaim the vibrant civic tradition in Minnesota.

In the next chapter, I describe the type of community practitioners necessary for this expansive model of education to be successful on a larger scale, before concluding with lessons and recommendations from the stories of Hull House, Highlander Folk School, and the Neighborhood Learning Community.

Chapter Six

Community Practitioners

The touchstones of the new practice are new professional skills, new professional norms, new power relations, and a new mind-set about what it means to be a professional.

—Lisbeth Schorr, *Common Purpose*

As the case of the Neighborhood Learning Community (NLC) clearly indicates, education today needs to be accompanied by new democratic skills, knowledge, values, and practices to support democratic renewal. As I explored the landscape of civic education, I discovered many "community practitioners" who embody these traits and are putting them into practice in communities around the United States. These are the people able to connect colleges and universities, schools, and communities in a way that develops the different kind of politics—a politics centered on citizens—described in the cases of Hull House, Highlander, and the NLC.

Think about the democratic habits and tools it took to imagine and organize a festival on the West Side of St. Paul that celebrates the contribution of immigrants, or a youth apprenticeship project that enables youth to get to know their communities through public work, or a school that allows immigrants to learn English through reciprocal learning with college students.

In many respects, these are not new habits or tools—they are similar to what it took to institute a "labor museum" for adult immigrants at the turn of the twentieth century in Chicago or the skills required for developing a new method of teaching adult African Americans to read in the Jim Crow South. And while they are not the dominant approach learned by many in our now more specialized society that often teaches people to "go by the book" rather than trust instincts or be creative, these are the habits and skills that must be learned by today's community practitioners if we are to use the community as a place to effectively educate for democracy.

Community practitioners are sometimes described as new practitioners, community builders, public workers, or community connectors.[1] While community practitioners are often professionals staffed within institutions—such as schools, colleges, community centers, health centers, professional offices—they are able to see the public dimensions of their positions and are not stifled by the narrow professional "expert-driven" tendency of many institutional positions, norms, or cultures. In short, community practitioners are reformers who are able to connect education in the community with civic engagement by developing and utilizing new democratic habits and new democratic tools.

New Democratic Habits

I discovered three primary habits that most distinguish community practitioners who connect education in the community and civic engagement in my interviews and research. First, community practitioners are reflective practitioners who are able to "think-in-action." In this process, they are forced to master the art of improvisation—they listen, learn, and react to situations on the spot. Second, community practitioners are community connectors who link the diverse worlds of community learning with action for political change. This is done, mostly, by strategically linking people and institutions to build new alliances. Finally, community practitioners utilize multiple fields of education. Specifically, community practitioners find ways to work within the structures of informal as well as formal education.

Thinking-in-Action

Realizing that the areas of expertise required of today's professional practitioners lie beyond conventional practices learned in school, Donald Schön is most well known for developing a new epistemology of practice based on how professionals think-in-action. Schön's "reflective practitioners" are professionals who go beyond theories or techniques; these practitioners are able to invent ways of knowing and acting that are more artful than scientific. Thus, the actions of practitioners are responsible not only for the application of knowledge, but also for its generation.[2]

These skills are often difficult to explain. There is, as Schön writes, "no satisfactory way of describing or accounting for the artful competence which practitioners sometimes reveal in what they do."[3] To competently deal with cases that fall outside of existing theories and frameworks, a community practitioner must use the power of improvisation: inventing and testing in the situation strategies of their own devising.[4]

Community practitioners might best be compared with jazz musicians because of these improvisational talents. Like the jazz musician who knows how to improvise in playing a musical composition, so the community practitioner must know how to improvise in building relationships, responding to problems, and organizing for positive change. They must build on people's unique experiences and seek opportunities for creative intervention.

The stories in this book highlight the importance of both detail and particulars, but also messiness and improvisation. Innovative projects most often develop through the spontaneous responses of community practitioners' thinking-in-action, as the founding and development of Hull House, Highlander Folk School, and the Jane Addams School on the West Side of St. Paul each demonstrate.

Connecting Diverse Communities

A second important habit for community practitioners is connectivity: the ability to link the many places where people spend time. Community practitioners are able to see the work they do in the context of the communities where they work, and are deeply committed to connecting different community systems.

This connective role is essential for today's educators as well, who must do much more than simply "teach." Educators must act as connectors by building bridges across diverse communities and catalyzing participation among diverse stakeholders. Jerome Stein, himself, is a master community practitioner, writes: "Our educators often become community builders, or community connectors—people who build bridges between (and gain participation from) the stakeholders in a community."[5]

In the widely acclaimed book, *The Tipping Point*, Malcolm Gladwell introduces his readers to the benefits of "weak ties" for making social change through a series of stories about effective community connectors who have relationships with a varied and diverse group of people. Gladwell chronicles people like Lois Weisberg, the commissioner of Cultural Affairs for the City of Chicago, a community practitioner who is remarkably able to connect people from the diverse worlds of artists and musicians, to politicians and lawyers, to environmentalists and activists. Gladwell notes, "Connectors . . . are extraordinary people. We rely on them to give us access to opportunities and worlds to which we don't belong."[6]

To illustrate this point, Gladwell recalls a study in the late 1960s by Stanley Milgram on how human beings are connected to one another. Milgram's idea was to test how people are connected with a simple chain letter. He randomly selected 160 people from Omaha, Nebraska, and mailed them a packet that included the name and address of a Boston stockbroker who lived in Sharon, Massachusetts. The subjects were asked to write their names on a roster and send the package to someone they thought would be closer to the stockbroker. Milgram found that most of the letters arrived in five or six steps—demonstrating the concept "six degrees of separation." More interestingly, half of the packages that arrived were delivered to the stockbroker by three people at the end of the chain. Gladwell observes, "Six degrees of separation doesn't mean that everyone is linked to everyone else in just six steps. It means that a very small number of people are linked to everyone else in a few steps, and the rest of us are linked to the world through those special few."[7]

In both historical and contemporary examples of community-based civic education, the people who are linked to a large number of people in a few steps are the community connectors. People like Lois Weisberg, or, say, Leonard Covello at Benjamin Franklin High School, Septima Clark of the Highlander Folk School, Jane Addams at Hull House, or the "community connector" staff position in the NLC use this democratic habit to navigate power, connect multiple worlds, recognize community assets, create community, and practice democratic education.

Using Informal Education

Often the location of the educational efforts of community practitioners is beyond the boundaries of the classroom in an area of study that has been termed "informal education." Informal education "involves seeking to foster learning in the situations where we work. It entails cultivating environments in which people are able to remember significant experiences, and to work at understanding them. It also means creating new situations where people can experience new things."[8]

Informal education is outside the classroom, voluntary, and occurs in multiple community settings. It also happens throughout any neighborhood, in places like coffee shops, Laundromats, restaurants, local businesses, and other "hangouts," as well as in public institutions, such as libraries and museums. Informal learning also occurs within recreation centers, playgrounds, community centers, community gardens, religious institutions, and community-based organizations, with activities that often include the creation of public art such as community murals and community photography. It can be captured in oral histories. And informal education occurs through cultural rituals and artwork such as storytelling, dancing, weaving, and sewing.

This community learning tends to value wisdom based on experience, as opposed to credentialized knowledge. At its best, however, informal education becomes a seamless voice in the cacophony of teaching and learning. This is what happened, for example, at Benjamin Franklin High School in East Harlem in the 1930s.

Leonard Covello's educational philosophy rested on the claim that for a school to fulfill its purpose it must become a center of the community life in its neighborhood. But Covello also found that informal learning activities often more easily sparked the interest of students. This experienced principal recognized that a successful school "cannot function as a detached organization concerned only with the imparting of book knowledge to a fluctuating number of pupils during a specified number of hours daily through a limited period each year." Covello continued:

> Closing bells must not be a signal of release for school and teacher as well as for the pupil. Education does not cease automatically on the stroke of the gong each afternoon. As a matter of fact, the closing bell merely admits the child into a different educational field, that of the community itself, where learning is aided by a vivid interest that is, unfortunately, seldom perceptible in the ordinary classroom.[9]

Thus, Covello is an impressive example of a community practitioner who not only was able to think-in-action and be a community connector, but also believed that education took place beyond the classroom.

A Contemporary Example:
The Community Connector

A more contemporary example of these democratic habits comes from the NLC and the job of the "community connector." This position was held at first by Kari Denissen, a young organizer who first participated in the Jane Addams School, interned at the Kettering Foundation, and then became the first Community Connector with the NLC. When asked about this unique position, Denissen answered: "This is always the hardest question. Whenever people 'What do you do?' I don't know how to explain it. I think it's because we had to make up what this job is. There isn't a strict job description. It evolves and changes based on what's needed."[10] This response recalls the multitude of democratic habits and techniques needed for community practitioners previously described, which Jerome Stein observes as an emerging type of practitioner. Stein explains:

One of the ways you can spot [community practitioners] is that if you ask them what they do, they often don't know how to answer you. And they'll tell you that, "Well, you know, I work at the park after school, but I'm going to collaboration meetings at City Hall, and I'm meeting with this neighborhood group and writing grants and it seems like if I tell you I work at the park it doesn't describe what I do."[11]

The practitioners described by Stein and the work of the Community Connector on the West Side are also reminiscent of what Jane Addams termed the "commission work" done by Hull House residents and the efforts by Highlander staff to understand a community with whom they were working.

Moreover, the development of many of the NLC partnerships, for example, emerged from relationships built by simply spending time with people and programs at other West Side organizations. When her work first began, Denissen visited the local 4-H program and soon began to co-lead a youth group each week for several months. The time devoted to building relationships eventually led to a number of partnerships with 4-H. A 4-H organizer admits, "It's important to have people like [the Community Connector] because she has time to do relationship building. I can only spend so much time on relationship building."[12] This relationship eventually helped inspire the idea of having youth do paid work of public significance in the community as part of the Youth Apprenticeship Project.

New Democratic Tools

The relational work done by the community connector also calls on community practitioners to employ a new set of democratic tools. Community practitioners, it seems, develop a set of democratic skills for success, including community assets mapping, community power mapping, and "being local." These tools, however, differ from technocratic techniques in that they are meant to generate local knowledge and provide for inclusion, rather than impose rigidity or uniformity.[13]

Community Assets Mapping

John McKnight and John Kretzmann of the Asset-Based Community Development Institute at Northwestern University have done the most over the past two decades to shift the emphasis in community development and professional practice from a focus on community "deficits" to a focus on community "assets." This shift is increasingly necessary due to the rise of the helping professionals industry—professionals hired to fix the problems in communities, problems that their jobs are dependent on. McKnight and Kretzmann argue that when looking at a neighborhood, especially a low-income, urban neighborhood, trained professionals tend to evaluate its needs and deficiencies. These "experts," accordingly, tend to enter neighborhoods from the outside and emphasize problems like abandoned buildings, drugs, and gangs.[14]

McKnight and Kretzmann offer another approach. Instead of looking at needs and deficits, they suggest that educators and organizers look at the gifts and assets within a neighborhood. Like Leonard Covello did with youth in East Harlem, and Jane Addams and others did in Chicago with *Hull House Maps and Papers*, McKnight and Kretzmann suggest a philosophical stance and a community-building technique known as "community assets mapping."

Kretzmann and McKnight suggest that community assets mapping be conducted on multiple levels by compiling an inventory of the gifts of individuals (e.g., skills, talents), citizens' associations (e.g., churches, block clubs), and local institutions (e.g., schools, businesses). These are compiled by going person-to-person, household-to-household, building-to-building, and block-to-block asking questions and listening to people in their life-situations. In this process, there in a paradigmatic shift: people are seen not as problems to be fixed, but as capable and creative citizens. Moreover, the act of mapping itself is a community building opportunity that builds a new network of relationships and, ultimately, helps develop educative communities.

Community Power Mapping

Building citizen capacity has been the primary work of co-directors Harry Boyte and Nan Skelton and their colleagues at the Center for Democracy and Citizenship at the University of Minnesota for more than a decade. The Center for Democracy and Citizenship works to develop the theory and practice of "what works" to engage citizens in democracy. These efforts have helped them create language and practice that conceives of citizens not as passive "clients" or "consumers," but as powerful "producers" and "creators" of their lives and communities.[15]

The Center for Democracy and Citizenship has developed a practical philosophy of "public work," the sustained, visible, and serious efforts by a diverse mix of ordinary people that creates things of lasting civic or public significance. An example of public work, often cited by Boyte, was the creative efforts of the Civilian Conservation Corps in the 1930s. Many other examples have been described in this study.

The Center for Democracy and Citizenship is a primary partner in the NLC and has initiated a youth citizenship initiative, Public Achievement. In Public Achievement, teams of young people ranging from elementary school to college work over a period of months on a public issue of their choice. Much like the students at Covello's community school in East Harlem, Public Achievement enables young people to initiate public work projects on issues they care about. They work with adult coaches to combat issues such as violence, teen pregnancy, racism, and educational inequality. This approach has spread to hundreds of American and international communities, including Northern Ireland, South Africa, and Turkey. One example, a group of youths working to reform the U.S. citizenship exam, was detailed in chapter five.

A core tool for this work is "community power mapping." In Public Achievement, for example, teams of young people work with an adult coach to address selected issues by power mapping: strategically analyzing the power, connections, and diverse interests and then building public relationships with key stakeholders. Public Achievement groups ask questions, such as, "Who has an interest in this issue?" They then probe further, asking: "What is their interest?" Youth then often conduct "one-on-one" meetings that help them gain a greater appreciation and understanding for the complexity of an issue and find areas of common ground.

Power mapping introduces the importance of the issues of "power" and "self-interest" for community practitioners, building on the lessons from community organizers such as Saul Alinsky and the Industrial Areas Foundation, and Dorothy Cotton and the Citizenship Schools of the civil rights movement. In the process, civic knowledge is acquired, along with powerful community alliances. Power mapping, in short, helps people develop the knowledge and relationships so important to be effective in making community change.

Being Local

The processes of community asset and power mapping inevitably lead to not only new sets of relationships, but also a different lens on the local situation. In *Local Education*, Mark Smith uses a series of interviews with community educators to define local education. Localness means, in the words of one of these educators, "reaching out to people on their own patch, territory, call it what you want; and initiating projects where they are at." Smith then concludes, "For the most part this entails working with or within local institutions, networks and practices: enhancing relationships and practices."[16]

This form of education defines another important tool for community practitioners: being local.[17] A community practitioner describes this approach in *Local Education:* "[Being local] involves learning in detail about the participants in practice, their lives, their histories, and their relationships to one another. It includes learning the characteristics that define a place: family, neighborhood, community, culture. It also includes learning aspects of the physical world defining a place."[18]

Similarly, in a curriculum for youth workers on this approach, Jerome Stein writes, "Being local helps youth workers stay grounded in their organizations or communities. In the same way that skilled youth workers know how to pay attention and really listen to individual kids and youth, being local is about learning how to listen and pay attention to communities and community organizations."[19] Being local is a skill used for community connection, often between educational institutions and local communities.

One of the ways community practitioners are local is simply be walking around and "being about." Being about involves activities such as "walking round the estate, visiting local launderettes, cafes, chip shops, pubs, and even wandering into the school at break and lunch times," Smith writes. "The aim generally is to be seen, to make and maintain contact with client groups, and to undertake work as it [arises]."[20] Educators, in this model, create opportunities for conversations in ordinary settings and develop the ability to get closer to the pulse of a community.

Localness often appears in unlikely places, like the office of a university president. For example, Robert Scott, president of Adelphi University, describes how he reached out to the experiences of students by doing three things not often undertaken by a college president: living on campus in a student dormitory, taking a freshman seminar designed to orient students to university opportunities, and co-teaching a class in ethics.

By getting to know the university from different perspectives, Scott built new relationships and discovered things about the university most college presidents would never see. For instance, in the freshman seminar he asked a fellow student where she stashed her books in between classes and when she replied "my car," he soon learned that the school only had twenty lockers for more than 5,000 commuter students. In describing his experience living with students, Scott says he "learned about [students] as individuals, the setting in which they lived and studied, their network of friends, their relationships to faculty and staff, and their challenges in navigating the Ramapo campus and curriculum."[21]

There are also many examples of being local in the cases presented in this book. For instance, Septima Clark argued that Highlander's Citizenship Schools is based on the belief that creative local leaders are present in every community and they simply need to be discovered and developed. Thus, the schools, according to Clark, needed to have the "ability to adapt at once to specific situations and stay in the local picture only long enough to help in the development of local leaders."[22] The Citizenship Schools, in short, worked to cultivate and teach localness among community leaders.

Clark's observations are similar to the efforts by the "community connector" for the NLC when she simply spent time visiting local community organizations, looking for ways that partnerships might arise organically. And the many narratives of people in the Chicago neighborhood around Hull House or local leaders who came to Highlander are an embodiment of being local.

Being local is also a something I attempted to do in listening to the stories and practices for this book. I attempted to learn in detail about the participants, practices, histories, relationships, and characteristics that define Hull House, Highlander Folk School, and the Neighborhood Learning Community. I examine the lessons from these cases in the final chapter.

Chapter Seven

Conclusion
Taking It Home

[The ecology of education] must now move beyond description to prescription. . . . Prescribing an education that addresses all aspects of a
child's life and deliberately connects formal school with its larger surround will require a grand leap of imagination. Indeed the very way I
describe the prospect—"connecting formal school with its surround"—
is constricting in that my picture implies a 'place' with satellites. That
will no longer do.

—Theodore Sizer, *The Red Pencil*

The case studies presented in this book are part of what researchers who
study the everyday life of communities describe as the "steady, but always
changing commitment to study human experience from the ground up,
from the point of interacting individuals who, together and alone, make
and live the histories that have been handed down from the ghosts of the
past."[1] When this is done, when we examine human experiences from
the ground up, new ideas are sure to emerge. This book illuminates new
ways of thinking about politics and education. At the same time, important, and often forgotten, older traditions reemerge. In my research I
found that the ghosts of the past, from places like Hull House and Highlander, are alive in contemporary efforts, like those of the Neighborhood
Learning Community.

   This gives me great hope. It tells me that putting American education back into balance is within our reach. It is possible to view education
more expansively, utilizing and connecting the multiple institutions that
educate. It is also possible to connect learning in the community with
democratic practice. But making this happen on a broader scale will require a longer view and a different kind of politics led by bold citizens
and innovative civic institutions.[2]

127

I have argued throughout that schools are important, but that community must also be a vehicle for civic learning. Community, of course, is also no panacea. Like schools, communities have challenges and many community-based organizations themselves operate within a professionalized, deficit-based model. And yet the cases I studied indicate that communities can provide an essential context for educating for democracy.

Lessons Learned

It seems evident that the problems of community deterioration, democratic disengagement, and academic underperformance are not being successfully addressed by government policy, schooling, or by other potential mediating institutions, such as colleges, universities, or community-based institutions. It is also apparent that these interrelated issues cannot be addressed by any of these institutions in isolation. Therefore, Ira Harkavy, one of the most articulate voices for what I term the ecology of civic learning, calls for systemic reform and puts forward a challenge for educators and policy makers:

> A strategy needs to be developed that connects school and school system change to a process of *democratic* community change and development. The strategy should be directed toward tapping, integrating, mobilizing, and galvanizing the enormous untapped resources of communities, including colleges and universities, for the purpose of improving schooling and community life.[3]

The foundation for such a strategy is evident in this study, based on an approach that advances the ecology of civic learning.

An analysis of Hull House, Highlander Folk School, and the Neighborhood Learning Community (NLC) gives greater meaning to this model, which entails looking at the ways education in the community and civic engagement overlap to educate for democracy. These cases produce ideas and real-world examples on connecting education with civic life. And the lessons learned from the cases in this study include:

- Commit to making change over longer periods of time,
- Place a deliberate emphasis on comprehensive, relational, and public education,
- Make learning relevant to people's everyday lives,
- Recognize the creative powers of diversity through public work,
- Utilize the talents and instincts of nonprofessionals,
- Foster reciprocal relationships,
- Embrace flexibility and trust in the messiness of democracy.

Change Requires Time

Robert Halpern has written a history of neighborhood initiatives as responses to poverty and social problems. One conclusion of his study is that most often "reform impulses in America are short-lived."[4] New generations must deal with the unfulfilled promises and tasks of prior generations. As we look at the history of educational responses to social problems, there is an impulse toward the short-term program and solution, not the long-term effort. This is confirmed from my case study research on civic education. Again and again, I found that *time* is an essential variable for education in the community to connect with civic engagement. Horton's autobiography, aptly titled *The Long Haul*, seems a fitting description for this lesson.

Jane Addams at Hull House, Myles Horton at Highlander, and leaders in the Neighborhood Learning Community such as Nan Skelton, Nan Kari, D'Ann Lesch, See Moua, Gunnar Liden, and Kari Denissen exemplify the importance of spending time building community. Their commitments illuminate that change does not happen in snapshots or with one-time programs; rather, change requires the deliberate and arduous commitment of time.

Horton founded Highlander in 1932, where he lived and worked for 58 years until his death in 1990. Jane Addams spent forty-six years at Hull House, from its founding in 1889 until her death in 1935. Aware of these extraordinary commitments, many of the leaders involved with the Neighborhood Learning Community have been participating since the founding of the Jane Addams School in 1996. Many of the children from the Jane Addams School have grown into leaders of the Neighborhood Learning Community. And college students have stayed involved throughout their years in college and beyond graduation; some have even settled in the West Side neighborhood.

Carrie Catt, a contemporary of Jane Addams, helps explain the importance of time when she eulogized that Jane Addams would head her list of the country's greatest women. "I do not base her greatness on Hull House," she explained at Addams's funeral, "important as that contribution is. Far more remarkable is the human trait of sticking to that project all her life. She made it a success. She stuck through when it was a success. That is a rare thing to do—to stick to a success."[5] Having educators willing to "stick to it" is essential for long-term civic change.

Comprehensive, Relational, Public Education

To include civic dimensions to learning requires a deliberate emphasis on *comprehensive, relational,* and *public* education.[6] Comprehensive, relational, and public learning, absent from many educational settings, is evident in the case studies I present. Hull House, Highlander, and the Neighborhood Learning Community act comprehensively by considering all the institutions that educate for democracy within the ecology of education—not simply classrooms. Education, therefore, includes community centers, nonprofits, libraries, museums, retreat centers, local businesses, as well as traditional schooling.

Hull House, Highlander, and the NLC act relationally by demonstrating the interconnections between the locations where education occurs. The NLC's West Side Circulator embodies this by making stops at many of the informal and formal places where education takes place in the neighborhood. The network also has a "community connector" who links the people and institutions that are part of the web of learning. Esau Jenkins played this role for the early Citizenship Schools on Johns Island by connecting the ideas of citizenship education with the many community organizations with which he was involved, including Highlander. Hull House residents also acted relationally, doing what Addams termed "commission work," connecting neighborhood residents with public institutions.

Finally, with civic learning, the primary goal is not simply private gain for the individual learners who participate. These cases illustrate how education can also help institutions—schools, colleges and universities, businesses, and community institutions—become more public spirited. In discussing its commission work, Jane Addams recognizes the impact Hull House had in helping other institutions move beyond individual "formulas" to connect with a broader, public mission.[7]

The NLC works with a series of institutions, such as the University of Minnesota and the Riverview Public Library, which have public missions that are often marginalized by the powerful privatizing forces of the broader consumer society. This educational network plays a mediating role to help institutions recapture public purpose. In my interviews with people involved with the NLC, for example, the local librarian claimed libraries can once again be "people's universities," and people associated with the University of Minnesota pledged to be "an architect for democracy" in supporting these efforts.

In its early work, Highlander helped democratize labor unions, and later worked with community institutions like black churches on civil rights—all with public aims. And efforts such as Highlander's support for the civil rights movement, Hull House's advocacy for child labor laws and sanitary streets, and the NLC's work for immigration and school reform demonstrate that education can transform publics as well as individuals.

Relevant Learning

Unlike much of the current focus on educational accountability measured by "one-size-fits-all" high-stakes testing, Hull House, Highlander, and the NLC emphasize making learning relevant to everyday life by respecting people's unique experiences. Experience, therefore, can be the touchstone for educative growth. This lesson might be summed up simply as: "engagement matters." When people are engaged in learning that is relevant to their lives, they want to learn more.

The learning circle approach used at Highlander (and by the Neighborhood Learning Community) recognizes that the best teachers of poor and working-class people are "the people themselves." Learners are the experts in their own stories, and they are most often best able to solve their own problems. The iron rule of community organizing applies to civic education—never do for others what they can do for themselves.

The role of a civic educator is to create free and open spaces for people to share experiences, learn from their peers, and, ultimately, act collectively. With this approach, educators find ways to build on stories using what Horton called his "two-eyed theory of education"—with one eye on people's experiences and another on their best aspirations— as discussed in chapter four. When learning is relevant, educators are more likely to "free the powers within people," as Jane Addams encouraged.[8] For Addams, important insights came from events—brief moments that exemplified larger insights. Addams used these experiences as the basis for reflective narratives, like the narrative of "Angelina Discovering Her Mother's Talents," related in chapter four, or the "Devil Baby" narrative at the core of *The Long Road of Woman's Memory*.[9] These event narratives in turn were also the basis for educational programs, such as the Labor Museum, the many art and theater classes, and public discussions that were hallmarks at Hull House. When educators pay attention to narratives, as Addams did, experiences can lead to empowering contextualized learning, which then can also become relevant to civic learning.

The practices of the NLC also illustrate that in a contemporary setting, especially when working with immigrant adults and youths, making learning relevant is essential. Education in the community is based on the premise that people's unique experiences are the foundation for democratic life. This was seen, for example, in the Youth Apprenticeship Project when young people often find that their work in the community was more relevant and connected to their lives than their experiences in school. Through reflections with university coaches, young people often argued that their work in the community was more connected with their cultures, identities, and interest in making change.

Creative Powers of Diversity

Hull House, Highlander Folk School, and the Neighborhood Learning Community each recognize the creative powers of diversity through common, public work. A public work approach respects the resources of cultural, gender, age, class, and racial differences by finding ways for diverse people to contribute to solving public problems. Diversity, then, is honored not as a token gesture, but as a contribution to the creation of democratic communities.

The mostly female residents of Hull House were committed to addressing problems in the neighborhood, whether they were essential needs or structural reform. Settlement workers put issues in a larger democratic context. In response to the forces of industrialization and the influx of non–English-speaking immigrants to fast-growing cities, settlement workers put new Americans in the position of leaders with projects such as the Labor Museum. This enabled immigrants to teach and then display their traditional craft skills. It also created public space for the skills and values of immigrants, helping their transmission to a new generation. Addams said from the beginning that Hull House was about creating a democracy that allows a diverse group of people to contribute their talents to the common lot. "This is the penalty of democracy," she writes in *Democracy and Social Ethics*, "that we are bound to move retrograde or forward together. None of us can stand aside."[10]

In the segregated South from the 1940s through 1960s, Highlander adds another important example of respecting the creative powers that black and white activists could have together in a nonsegregated setting. Beginning in the early 1940s, Highlander refused to accept the unjust segregation laws, and decided to host integrated workshops. On the issue of desegregation, the policy was clear: black and white students would learn together, eat meals together, sleep in the same room together, dance together, and be treated equally at Highlander. This practice had an impact on many people, including Rosa Parks, who discovered for the first time that people of different races could join together for justice and equality.

Involving diverse groups of people from different ages, cultures, classes, and races in common work is also paramount in the Neighborhood Learning Community. For example, Hmong, Latino, African, and European Americans create the annual Freedom Festival together. The creation of the festival itself embodies a celebration of democratic ideals. The festival highlights the distinct aspects of different cultures and includes a strong embrace of immigrant heritages. The community festival shows how racial and cultural differences in a neighborhood can be overcome through an intergenerational shared enterprise—in this case, the creation and actualizing of a community celebration about the shared desire for freedom.

When young people are given the opportunity to make public contributions, as is done with the NLC's Youth Apprenticeship Project, the creative power of diversity is also evident. A youth apprentice, for instance, reflects that an important lesson from the work with a diverse group, including college students, community residents, and teachers, is to be able to "see things from different perspectives."

Nan Kari, an organizer with the NLC, expands on this lesson: "The only way [the immense diversity] works is for people to learn a different kind of politics, to negotiate different interests and perspectives."[11] Thus, this "different kind of politics" (a public work approach) allows young people to navigate divisive and diverse communities with an appreciation for various perspectives. Like early settlement house residents or civil rights workers, these essential democratic skills help young people recognize the creative powers of diversity and be more effective democratic community practitioners.

Talents and Instincts of Nonprofessionals

Highlander, Hull House, and the NLC rely heavily on the talents and instincts of nonprofessionals in their educational endeavors. Perhaps the best example of this approach was when Myles Horton refused to hire certified teachers for the Citizenship Schools because he felt this type of professional training would cause people to impose their schooling methodology on the students. Thus, the Citizenship Schools hired a black beautician with no teaching experience, Bernice Robinson, as their first teacher. As further evidence of this lesson, the Citizenship Schools had the most difficulty in "degree-crazy" places, according to Septima Clark, where the credentializing presence of colleges and universities made community learning more difficult to promote.[12]

The settlement movement also relied on the talents and instincts of nonprofessionals. Hull House, for example, was "staffed" by settlement workers who lived and worked in the neighborhood. These residents came from mostly upper-class backgrounds, but they addressed issues as collaborators and co-investigators with their low-income neighbors. Addams's writing is filled with stories of Hull House residents tackling local politics, delivering babies, lobbying for reform, and advising both their immigrant neighbors and city leaders on a variety of issues—none of which they were formally trained or certified to do.[13]

Overcoming the tendency to rely on professionals to lead projects is much more difficult in our current technocratic society.[14] Well-meaning professionals, armed with credentials and standardized techniques, have come to dominate almost every sector of society—from social work and education to politics and business—and are especially prominent in knowledge-producing areas like higher education.

In the NLC, community residents are not seen as clients, but as leaders and teachers. The same approach applies to university students, who are not regarded as volunteers. For example, in describing how a group of college students created the Children's Circle at the Jane Addams School, John Wallace explained, "We don't trust [the college students who run the Children's Circle] because they have specialized knowledge. We trust in their spirit and their honesty and their ability to learn. We go with their instincts and abilities." Wallace, who helped develop the Jane Addams School and influenced the Neighborhood Learning Community, summarizes: "We're learning how non-professionals can work in a community-based way to create something subtle and powerful."[15]

Thus, "experts" play the role of supporting nonprofessionals to claim power for themselves. "Some of the people in this community were leaders in Laos, in Thailand, and in Latin America," explains NLC organizer Nan Skelton. "But many have not been able to translate that into leadership in relation to the incredibly complex world of the St. Paul school system."[16] With this insight in mind, NLC organizers initiated a series of trainings and workshops to help parents gain political skills to navigate the complex world of the public school system and help young people make positive changes in their schools and communities. One of the youths involved in this work explained what she learned from these trainings for promoting community engagement: "Get to know the community you are working with—the history, the people. Get to know lots of people. Before you start your own program, be with other programs in the same area, not as a volunteer, but just be with them for a while."[17] The simple lesson, it seems, is the essence of providing leadership opportunities for noncredentialed community residents, young and old.

Reciprocal Relationships

"At the Jane Addams School, everyone is a teacher and everyone is a learner," explained a graduate student from the Humphrey Institute voicing the stated philosophy of the school and the broader Neighborhood Learning Community. The student continued, "I found that even while I was primarily a teacher as we studied for the [naturalization] test, I still learned a lot. I mostly learned by trying to teach the concepts of freedom and democracy. Having to find ways to illustrate showed me how contextual they are, and challenged me to think of what they meant to me."[18] The importance of reciprocal relationships could have been voiced by residents of Hull House, those involved in the Youth Apprenticeship Project, teachers in the Citizenship Schools, or participants in countless civic learning projects.

The educational philosophy of Highlander helped to inspire the approach of the Neighborhood Learning Community, as it is common to hear the words of Bernice Robinson, the first teacher of the Citizenship Schools, in their educational efforts. Setting the tone in the first class in the back room of a cooperative store, Robinson said, "I am not a teacher; we are going to learn together. You are going to teach me as much as I'm going to teach you."[19]

This same spirit of reciprocal relationships was prominent at Hull House. Addams always said the settlement house experiment addressed mutual problems: the "objective" needs of the urban poor as well as the "subjective" desires of the privileged suffering from the paralysis of inaction. In fact, Addams insisted that she founded Hull House just as much for herself as the poor who lived in the neighborhood. Most significant, as a way to show that the settlement was not simply an act of charity, Addams often linked the need for reciprocal relationships to the promise of democracy. "[Hull House] is an effort to add the social function to democracy," explains Addams. "It was opened on the theory that the dependence of classes on each other is reciprocal; and that 'the social relationship is essentially a reciprocal relation.'"[20]

Flexibility and Trust in the Messiness of Democracy

Democracy is not a fixed point; as the case studies in this book illustrate, it is dynamic, ever-changing, and messy—a final lesson for connecting community and civic learning. For instance, the weekly reflection session with young people involved with the Youth Apprenticeship Project is a high-energy and often chaotic environment, with young people scattered around the room filled with excitement and sometimes wanting to talk all at once. The same could certainly be said of a learning circle at Highlander. These sessions are not held in traditional classrooms that have students sitting neatly in rows—nor should they be.

These community practitioners have learned not only to deal with messiness, but also to thrive in uncertainty. Their reform work requires a spirit of improvisation and adaptation that marks the creative longevity that Highlander and Hull House exemplify, along with the courage to try new things, seen with the Neighborhood Learning Community.

This approach also requires an unbending trust in the capacity of ordinary people. When Myles Horton declared that there is no method to learn at Highlander aside from "trusting people and believing in their ability to think for themselves," he meant that flexibility and trust are essential for democratic practice.[21] Early partners in the Neighborhood Learning Community also describe the need to trust people and be flexible, even though it will be messy. Recall, for example, John Wallace explaining their approach is simply to "trust the process" in the learning partnership in chapter five.

Flexibility is also seen in the responsiveness in each case study to community-generated requests. Highlander partnered at the request of Johns Island residents and later the requests of other communities to start Citizenship Schools. Organizers of the NLC tackle projects, such as teaching English, helping immigrants pass the naturalization exam, providing public neighborhood transportation, offering summer programming for the young, and trying to reform local schools because these were the community-defined issues, at those moments. Each of these actions was not predetermined; they were based on improvisational responses to the interests of the broader community.

Likewise, in a talk given in 1892, just after Hull House opened its doors, Jane Addams described the need for flexibility in the democratizing efforts of the settlement movement:

> The one thing to be dreaded in the Settlement is that it lose its flexibility, its power of quick adaptation, its readiness to change its methods as its environments may demand. . . . It must be hospitable and ready to experiment. . . . [Its residents] must be content to live quietly side by side with their neighbors until they grow into a sense of relationship and mutual interests. . . . In short, residents are pledged to devote themselves to the duties of good citizenship and to arousing of the social energies which too largely lie dormant in every neighborhood given over to industrialism.[22]

Addams, whose work responded to industrial conditions with agility and creativity, continues to provide good guidance today, as does Highlander; this approach is also seen in the Neighborhood Learning Community. The emphasis on narrative and relationship over statistics and programs in each of the three cases should impel us toward greater flexibility and trust in our civic efforts.

Recommendations

While advancing the connections between community, higher education, and schools, Ira Harkavy calls for an implementation of "the Noah Principle"—no more awards for predicting rain; prizes only for building the arks—a line appropriately borrowed from Louis Gerstner, former chairman of IBM.[23] How, then, do we build the arks that will enable us to effectively draw upon the vast resources of the community to educate for democracy?

Further research and multiple public dialogues are certainly part of the next steps for civic education. But it is also a time for public action. It will take organizing the multitude of often conflicting interests of stakeholders associated with education, including teachers' unions and teachers, administrators and school boards, parents and youth, community residents and community organizers, elected officials and policy makers, and college presidents, faculty, and college students. And it will involve altering power relationships among these stakeholders.[24] The following are some modest policy recommendations to contribute to this process and, ultimately, carrying out the lessons from this study.

Communities

First, and foremost, we need to document and share the lessons for community-based civic education efforts, such as those on the West Side of St. Paul (and in many other communities around the world), to create increased visibility and greater capacity for neighborhood learning communities to support civic learning. It seems evident that these partnerships should include collaborative networks among schools, colleges and universities, and community-based organizations. As the NLC illustrates, local ownership can help create successful community initiatives and public practices, including community-based youth apprenticeship projects with connections to school learning; trolleys circulating formal and informal community learning sites in the neighborhood; and community festivals in support of political achievement and local cultures.

Efforts can be designed to give local communities power in the form of funds. Specifically, foundations and government might invest in community-based organizations in a form of "reverse granting" to broker civic collaborations with schools, colleges, and universities, and provide mini-grants to youth and neighborhood residents for civic learning projects in the community.

A principle of these partnerships must always be reciprocity. This means that partnerships might include school–community councils, a community connector in every school in a school district, and school representatives on community boards. Community-based organizations might also work reciprocally on public problem-solving using learning circle retreats outside the community (as done at Highlander), and partner with local college students and faculty, as well as youth and K–12 schools, on community research and engagement (as done at Hull House and the Neighborhood Learning Community). Finally, it also seems important to make these endeavors visible and sustainable; thus, partnerships with local media and support from elected officials and policy makers are vital.

Schools

As the *Civic Missions of Schools* report indicates, schools have a vital role to play in civic learning. As the history of education in the community and the case studies show, schools can become anchors for community learning and civic engagement; they can use their educational mandate to make civic learning a more expansive endeavor. This includes giving young people decision-making power on school and community issues; involving parents as co-educators and co-learners in schooling; rethinking transportation routes for schools and communities using the West Side Circulator as a model; making public art, music, and community theater part of civic learning; and using the school building itself as a site for community learning and intergenerational public dialogues.

In addition, schools can partner with community organizations to help young people participate in civic learning by facilitating projects for youth to become aware of the assets and needs in their local communities. This might be implemented by providing community building trainings for young people to develop the civic skills of deliberative dialogue, facilitation, public speaking and listening, and collaboration, along with training on the skills of community assets mapping, community power mapping, and "being local." It could include having neighborhood youth conduct community mapping of the assets in their neighborhoods and then publicizing the assets through Web sites, photography, murals, and other visual arts. And schools could create opportunities for young people to work in teams addressing public issues of their choosing, as done in the youth citizenship project, Public Achievement.

Colleges and Universities

Colleges and universities have an important role to play in helping to mediate the ecology of civic learning. As a group of land-grant presidents declared in *Renewing the Covenant*, universities must act "not only as agents of democracy but also as its architects" by providing bridges between the civic aspirations of individuals and the public work of the broader world.[25]

Colleges and universities could use their unique positions to connect K–12 schools with communities in a number of specific ways. For instance, higher education can offer postsecondary courses for local high school students in "Community and Civic Leadership" fashioned on the course offered by Metropolitan State University in St. Paul to the Citizenship Group to reform the U.S. citizenship exam, as described in chapter five. In these courses, inner-city high school students with leadership potential who are struggling academically get an introduction to college, along with college credit, by taking a civic leadership course located on the college campus with a community-based learning component.

Next, colleges and universities can use their credentialing power to make civic education a larger part of the academic experience. Colleges and universities ought to create degree programs and certificates in "civic learning" in collaboration with service-learning programs. Programs that offer interdisciplinary majors or minors in public and community service seem best equipped to pilot this option, illustrating the untapped connection between service-learning and civic outcomes. Democratic habits—such as thinking-in-action, connecting diverse communities, and using informal education—and democratic techniques—such as community assets mapping, community power mapping, and "being local"—should be part of the curriculum to create a new generation of reflective and deliberative community practitioners.

Finally, colleges and universities can offer "Community and Civic Leadership" scholarships for high school students who have been involved in community-based civic learning in high school. These student scholars can also function as civic leadership teams at the college, using Bentley College, DePaul University, and Indiana University–Purdue University Indianapolis (IUPUI) as models, enabling these student leaders to also play significant roles in connecting their institutions with the community.[26] The scholarships would serve as an incentive for high schools to make civic learning a priority, not unlike the current emphasis on academics, along with community service and sports.

Taking It Home

Today, we stand at a crossroads. We can continue the dominant prescription for education. This model puts the school and school system at the center of civic education. Or we can shift to a different direction. This new path requires what Theodore Sizer calls "a grand leap of imagination" to advance the ecology of civic learning. It necessitates reaching beyond the schools into the messy world of communities. This approach sees the interconnections between school and community systems; it is intergenerational, and it deliberately promotes comprehensive, relational, and public dimensions of education.

What, then, is required to take this leap of imagination in education? The stories in this book illustrate that a shift in the educational landscape can occur as the result of past failure or inspiration.

Change Because of Past Failure

A shift of thinking may occur, for example, out of frustration with a broken system—when educators are forced to learn from failure or a series of mistakes. After Myles Horton and Septima Clark failed to develop a model for adult leadership training, they learned from this experience and then successfully partnered with Esau Jenkins on the Citizenship Schools in Johns Island. Learning from mistakes occurred for Hull House residents as well when they took on a more pronounced political agenda after their initial assumptions about needing to "culturally uplift" the poor were challenged. And it has happened with the NLC when community organizations began to find that sharing resources becomes more effective than competition through their youth summer programming (All Around the Neighborhood) and with the use of funds allotted to transportation (West Side Circulator).

It seems that change may simply be inevitable as a result of our past failures. There is an emerging recognition that schools and communities must be interconnected as a result of frustration with the impact of narrow school-focused reform efforts. This, of course, coincides with the necessity of addressing the increasingly savage inequalities between urban, largely minority schools and communities and the schools and communities of much of suburban America. Simply stated, our current educational paradigm is broken, at least partly, as a result of our failure to understand our problems as interrelated and consequently to address issues holistically and ecologically.

Change Because of Inspiration

A leap of imagination may also occur because of affirmation, the result of being inspired by witnessing a new or innovative approach. Jane Addams was inspired to launch Hull House after seeing a new approach that put young people's passions to work addressing pressing community problems in her visit to Toynbee Hall in London. John Dewey had a similar influence: his work with Hull House led to the conception of schools as centers of community life. When Myles Horton visited Hull House and then the Danish folk schools, he discovered models that would inspire the creation of what Jane Addams described as a "rural settlement house." Aware of each of these traditions and models, a group of community organizers set out to recreate the spirit of the early settlement house movement using the "learning circle" method of the Highlander Folk School on the West Side neighborhood of St. Paul, which eventually developed into the Neighborhood Learning Community.

This more positive reason to think change is possible is also relevant today. We can point to inspiring, innovative models for addressing the interrelated challenges of poverty, educational inequality, community deterioration, and democratic disengagement. Hull House and the Highlander Folk School offer guidance for how community has played a major role in civic education, while the Neighborhood Learning Community provides a contemporary example of democratic cultural change by connecting education to civic life. A simple awareness of these innovative models seems important for moving in a different direction.

There is ample evidence to believe change is possible. Just look at the inadequacies of our current systems to educate for democracy, especially for our youngest citizens. Surely, we must realize that in isolation any institution is powerless to make the necessary civic improvements. At the same time, there are also beacons showing us new ways to connect democracy, community, and education with cases like Hull House, Highlander, and the Neighborhood Learning Community. Regardless of whether we learn from our failures or become inspired by innovative possibilities, the conclusion remains the same: we need to think, practice, and act in a different way.

A Highlander-style learning circle workshop ends by asking people to reflect on a forward-looking question: *What are you going to do when you got back home?* This seems like an apt final question for this endeavor as well. Taking a new path premised on new ways of defining "education" itself may seem daunting in an age of high-stakes testing, with entrenched sets of interests invested in the status quo. "Scaling up" is never easy—all models are time, place, and context specific. And yet I believe that if we make a sustained commitment to civic education, we will find that community matters in educating for democracy.

The cases presented here illustrate that a shift in direction is possible. Taking a new path, however, involves rethinking where education takes place; seeing people of all ages, backgrounds, and professional status as educators and resources; thinking more comprehensively, relationally, and publicly about learning; developing neighborhood learning community networks; and making civic learning a public priority. All this can only be accomplished by making, and then maintaining, a commitment to creating educative communities in pursuit of democracy. There is much initial promise in this great democratic task.

Notes

Preface

1. For examples of the "civic renewal movement," see Harry C. Boyte, *Everyday Politics: Reconnecting Citizens and Public Life* (Philadelphia: University of Pennsylvania, 2004); Peter Levine, "Civic Renewal in America," *Philosophy and Public Policy Quarterly 26*, no.1/2 (Winter/Spring 2006): 2–12; and Carmen Sirianni and Lewis Friedland, *Civic Innovation in America: Community Empowerment, Public Policy, and the Movement for Civic Renewal* (Berkeley: University of California Press, 2001). See also Carmen Sirianni and Lewis Friedland, *The Civic Renewal Movement: Community-Building and Democracy in the United States* (Dayton: Kettering Foundation Press, 2005) and Cynthia Gibson's excellent paper, *Citizens at the Center: A New Approach to Civic Engagement*, commissioned by the Case Foundation in 2006.

2. Herman Blake used the phrase "listen eloquently" in a speech given at the Second Annual National Gathering of the Invisible College, Indianapolis, Indiana, in June 1996. The idea of research continuing a conversation, rather than discovering a truth, comes from Richard Rorty, *Philosophy and the Mirror of Nature* (Princeton: Princeton University Press, 1979) and from Niobe Way's book documenting the lives of teenagers, *Everyday Courage: The Lives and Stories of Urban Teenagers* (New York: New York University Press, 1998). For an analysis of the different epistemology recognized in community-based learning, see Parker Palmer, "Community, Conflict, and Ways of Knowing: Ways to Deepen our Educational Agenda," *Change 19* (September/October 1987): 20-25. Palmer writes that "epistemology is not a bloodless abstraction" and that the way we know has implications for the way we live. Donald Schön argues for the legitimacy of knowledge that is generated-in-action in "The New Scholarship Requires a New Epistemology," *Change* (November/December 1995): 27-34. I am grateful to John Saltmarsh for helping me better understand the epistemological issues when community is seen as a legitimate source of knowledge creation.

Chapter One

Epigraph from John Dewey, *The School and Society* (Chicago: University of Chicago Press, 1990/1899), p. 34.

1. Stephen Macedo et al., *Democracy at Risk: How Political Choices Undermine Citizen Participation, and What We Can Do About It* (Washington, D.C.: Brookings Institution Press, 2005). The concerns about democracy have also been raised by the National Commission on Civic Renewal, *A Nation of Spectators: How Civic Disengagement Weakens America and What We Can Do About It* (College Park: University of Maryland, 1998); *The Civic Mission of Schools* (New York: Carnegie Corporation and Center for Information and Research on Civic Learning and Engagement, 2003); Scott Keeter et al., *The Civic and Political Health of the Nation: A Generational Portrait* (College Park, Maryland: Center for Information and Research on Civic Learning and Engagement, 2002); William Galston, "Political Knowledge, Political Engagement, and Civic Education," *Annual Review of Political Science 4* (2001) 217–234; and Robert Putnam, *Bowling Alone: The Collapse and Revival of American Community* (New York: Simon and Schuster, 2000).

2. Lawrence Cremin, *Public Education* (New York: Basic Books, 1976), p. 3.

3. National Commission on Civic Renewal, *A Nation of Spectators: How Civic Disengagement Weakens America and What We Can Do About It* (College Park: University of Maryland, 1998), p. 6.

4. This impressive organizing achievement was led by Peter Levine, the director of CIRCLE, and Cynthia Gibson, then a program officer at Carnegie Corporation. Gibson and Levine were the primary authors of *The Civic Mission of Schools* (New York: Carnegie Corporation and Center for Information and Research on Civic Learning and Engagement, 2003). Written and endorsed by more than sixty prominent scholars and education practitioners, *The Civic Mission of Schools* report summarizes the status of and need for civic learning in schools, kindergarten through twelfth grade. It analyzes trends in American political and civic engagement; articulates goals for civic education; demonstrates why schools are important venues for civic education; identifies promising approaches to educating students for democracy; and offers recommendations for revitalizing civic life to educators, policymakers, government officials, and funders.

5. *The Civic Mission of Schools* (New York: Carnegie Corporation and Center for Information and Research on Civic Learning and Engagement, 2003), p. 5.

6. The evidence for this began with "The Coleman Report," James Coleman, *Equality of Educational Opportunity* (Washington, D.C.: U.S. Office of Education, 1966). Later, the significance of schooling was questioned by Lawrence Steinberg, *Beyond the Classroom: Why School Reform Has Failed and What Parents Need To Do* (New York: Simon and Schuster, 1996) and James Traub, "What No School Can Do," *New York Times Magazine,* January 16, 2000. See also John I. Goodlad, *In Praise of Education* (New York: Teachers College Press, 1997).

7. This quote was told to me by David Mathews, president of the Kettering Foundation, where Lawrence Cremin served on the board of directors. See David

Mathews, *Reclaiming Public Education by Reclaiming our Democracy* (Dayton: Kettering Foundation Press, 2006).

8. Lawrence Cremin, *Public Education* (New York: Basic Books, 1976), p. 29.

9. Jane Addams, *Twenty Years at Hull House* (New York: Penguin Books, 1998/1910), p. 275.

10. For a discussion of the commodification of higher education, see Lee Benson and Ira Harkavy, "Saving the Soul of the University: What Is to be Done?," in *The Virtual University? Information, Markets, and Managements*, eds. Kevin Robins and Frank Webster (New York: Oxford University Press, 2001). For a powerful indictment of the segregation of schools and communities, see Jonathan Kozol, *Savage Inequalities: Children in America's Schools* (New York: Harper Perennial, 1991) and Jonathon Kozol, *The Shame of the Nation: The Restoration of Apartheid Schooling in America* (New York: Crown, 2005).

11. See Harry Boyte's excellent book for a detailed discussion of the possibility for a citizen-centered democracy, *Everyday Politics: Reconnecting Citizens and Public Life* (Philadelphia: University of Pennsylvania, 2004).

12. See the review of college student political engagement Ross Meyer and I conducted for CIRCLE and the Kettering Foundation, Nicholas V. Longo and Ross P. Meyer, "College Students and Politics: A Literature Review," CIRCLE Working Paper 46 (College Park, Maryland: Center for Information and Research on Civic Learning and Engagement, May 2006). See also *The Civic Mission of Schools* (New York: Carnegie Corporation and Center for Information and Research on Civic Learning and Engagement, 2003); Scott Keeter et al., *The Civic and Political Health of the Nation: A Generational Portrait* (College Park, Maryland: Center for Information and Research on Civic Learning and Engagement, 2002); William Galston, "Political Knowledge, Political Engagement, and Civic Education," *Annual Review of Political Science 4* (2001) 217–234; and Robert Putnam, *Bowling Alone: The Collapse and Revival of American Community* (New York: Simon and Schuster, 2000).

13. John I. Goodlad, *In Praise of Education* (New York: Teachers College Press, 1997), p. 41.

14. Lawrence Cremin uses "ecology of education" to describe the many places where learning occurs and the relationships between those places—or configurations—in *Public Education* (New York: Basic Books, 1976). He also applies this to civic learning, for example, in analyzing the lessons of Jane Addams and Hull House. Cremin states, "In a socialized democracy, the community itself would become educative in the diurnal business of contending with public issues and solving public problems." Cremin then concludes, "And out of the process would come a continually evolving definition of the common good" in *The Metropolitan Experience 1876–1980* (New York: Harper and Row, 1988), p. 179.

15. This definition of ecology comes from Wikipedia; see http://en.wikipedia.org/wiki/Ecology#The_ecosystem_concept.

16. I am grateful to Ross Meyer for helping me better understand the application of the concept of "ecology" to educating for democracy.

17. Cynthia Gibson, "From Inspiration to Participation: A Review of Perspectives on Youth Civic Engagement" (New York: Grantmaker Forum on Community and National Service, 2001). The former program officer for the Strengthening U.S. Democracy area of the Carnegie Corporation, Gibson wrote this report out of frustration with the lack of coordination among the various approaches to fostering youth civic engagement. It eventually led to the *Civic Mission of Schools* report.

18. This comes from many conversations with Harry Boyte. See especially Harry Boyte, "Public Work: Civic Populism Versus Technocracy in Higher Education," to be published by the Kettering Foundation.

19. *A Nation at Risk* (Washington, D.C.: The National Commission on Excellence in Education), p. 5.

20. Some of the central findings of the report, however, have since been called into question and the report is seen by many educators as the beginning of the standards-based movement. See Deborah Meier, "Educating a Democracy: Standards and the Future of Public Education," *Boston Review* (February/March 2000) and Richard Rothstein, *The Way We Were? The Myths and Realities of America's Student Achievement* (New York: Century Foundation Press, 1998).

21. Diane Ravitch, *Left Back: A Century of Battles over School Reform* (New York: Simon and Schuster, 2000), p. 414.

22. Jonathon Kozol, *Savage Inequalities: Children in America's Schools* (New York: Harper Perennial, 1991) and Jonathon Kozol, *The Shame of the Nation: The Restoration of Apartheid Schooling in America* (New York: Crown, 2005).

23. William Julius Wilson, *The Truly Disadvantaged* (Chicago: University of Chicago Press, 1987).

24. William Julius Wilson, *When Work Disappears: The World of the New Urban Poor* (New York: Vintage Books, 1996).

25. James Coleman, *Equality of Educational Opportunity* (Washington, D.C.: U.S. Office of Education, 1966). See also James Traub, "What No School Can Do," *New York Times Magazine,* January 16, 2000.

26. James Coleman, "Social Capital in the Creation of Human Capital," *American Journal of Sociology* 94 (1998): S95–S120, and James Coleman, *Foundations of Social Theory* (Cambridge: Harvard University Press, 1990).

27. Robert Putnam, "Bowling Alone: America's Declining Social Capital," *Journal of Democracy* 6 (1995): 65–78.

28. Robert Putnam, *Bowling Alone: The Collapse and Revival of American Community* (New York: Simon and Schuster, 2000).

29. Robert Putnam, "Community-Based Social Capital," *Making Good Citizens,* eds. Diane Ravitch and Joseph Viteritti (New Haven: Yale University Press, 2001), p. 87.

30. On the decline in political engagement, see, for example, *The Civic Mission of Schools* (New York: Carnegie Corporation and Center for Information and Research on Civic Learning and Engagement, 2003); William Galston, "Political Knowledge, Political Engagement, and Civic Education," *Annual Review of Political Science 4* (2001): 217–234; Scott Keeter et al., *The Civic and Political Health of the Nation: A Generational Portrait* (College Park, Maryland: Center for Information

and Research on Civic Learning and Engagement, 2002); and Robert Putnam, *Bowling Alone: The Collapse and Revival of American Community* (New York: Simon and Schuster, 2000).

31. National Commission on Civic Renewal, *A Nation of Spectators: How Civic Disengagement Weakens America and What We Can Do About It* (College Park: University of Maryland, 1998), p. 6.

32. National Association of Secretaries of State, *The New Millennium Project: Part I American Youth Attitudes on Politics, Citizenship, Government, and Voting* (Washington, D.C.: National Association of Secretaries of State, 1999).

33. Thomas Patterson, *The Vanishing Voter: Public Involvement in the Age of Uncertainty* (Cambridge: Knopf, 2002), p. 21.

34. Linda Sax et al., *The American Freshman: National Norms for Fall 2003* (Los Angeles: Higher Education Research Institute, UCLA Graduate School of Education and Information Studies, 2003). See also William Galston, "Political Knowledge, Political Engagement, and Civic Education," *Annual Review of Political Science 4* (2001): 217–234; and William Galston, "Civic Knowledge, Civic Education, and Civic Engagement: A Summary of Recent Research," in *Constructing Civic Virtue: A Symposium on the State of American Citizenship* (Syracuse, N.Y.: Campbell Public Affairs Institute, 2003). This section also draws on the research of Ross Meyer; see Nicholas V. Longo and Ross P. Meyer, "College Students and Politics: A Literature Review," CIRCLE Working Paper 46 (College Park, Maryland: Center for Information and Research on Civic Learning and Engagement, May 2006).

35. The concept of education being comprehensive, relational, and public comes from Lawrence Cremin, *Public Education* (New York: Basic Books, 1976).

36. For a good overview of the landscape of civic engagement in higher education, see "Engaged Campus" in Carmen Sirianni and Lewis Friedland, *The Civic Renewal Movement: Community-Building and Democracy in the United States* (Dayton: Kettering Foundation Press, 2005).

37. This comes from John Saltmarsh, who has been one of the most influential national proponents of the civic renewal movement in higher education. See John Saltmarsh, "The Civic Promise of Service-Learning," *Liberal Education* (Spring 2005).

38. Carmen Sirianni and Lewis Friedland, *Civic Innovation in America: Community Empowerment, Public Policy, and the Movement for Civic Renewal* (Berkeley: University of California Press, 2001). See also Carmen Sirianni and Lewis Friedland, *The Civic Renewal Movement: Community-Building and Democracy in the United States* (Dayton: Kettering Foundation Press, 2005); Lisbeth Schorr, *Common Purpose: Strengthening Families and Neighborhoods to Rebuild America* (New York: Anchor Books, 1997); Harry C. Boyte and Nan Kari, *Building America: The Democratic Promise of Public Work* (Philadelphia: Temple University Press, 1996); Harry C. Boyte, *Everyday Politics: Reconnecting Citizens and Public Life* (Philadelphia: University of Pennsylvania, 2004); and Peter Levine, "Civic Renewal in America," *Philosophy and Public Policy Quarterly 26*, no.1/2 (Winter/Spring 2006): 2–12.

39. Jerome Stein, "Youth Development in Context: Education in the Community," in *The University and the Community: Renewing the Relationship*, eds. Jerome Stein and Nicholas V. Longo (Minneapolis: Center for 4–H Youth Development, University of Minnesota, 2001), p. 12. The concept "education in the community" was developed by Jerome Stein at the University of Minnesota, where he teaches a course with this title. Separately, the term is used by Mark Smith in Britain to describe his informal education approach. See Mark Smith, "The Possibilities of Public Life: Educating in the Community," In *Education and Community: The Politics of Practice,* eds. Garth Allen and Ian Martin (New York: Cassell Education Series, 1992).

40. I provide an overview of the history of place-based education in an article with Ira Harkavy; see Ira Harkavy and Nicholas V. Longo, "Problem-Solving with Local Communities: Using University-Community-School Partnerships and Place-Based Education to Help Revitalize Urban America," *Democracy and Education 16*, no. 2 (2006): 16–23.

41. James Scott, *Seeing Like a State. How Certain Schemes to Improve the Human Condition Have Failed* (New Haven: Yale University Press, 1998), p. 6.

42. See Ira Harkavy and Marty Blank, "Community Schools: A Vision of Learning that Goes Beyond Testing," *Education Week*, April 17, 2002.

43. Ira Harkavy and Marty Blank, "Community Schools: A Vision of Learning that Goes Beyond Testing," *Education Week*, April 17, 2002, p. 38.

44. *The Civic Mission of Schools* (New York: Carnegie Corporation and Center for Information and Research on Civic Learning and Engagement, 2003), p. 4.

45. John Saltmarsh, "The Civic Promise of Service-Learning," *Liberal Education* (Spring 2005).

46. Theodore Sizer, *The Red Pencil: Convictions from Experience in Education* (New Haven: Yale University Press, 2004), p. 24.

47. For example, Harry Boyte argues that there are different implications for different political frameworks and differentiates three distinct approaches to civic education: "civics," "service," and "populism" in "Civic Education and the New American Patriotism Post-9/11," *Cambridge Journal of Education 33* (2003): 85-100. Joel Westheimer and Joseph Kahne detail three conceptions of the "good citizen"—personally responsible, participatory, and justice oriented— that underscore political implications of education for democracy in "Educating the 'Good' Citizen: The Politics of School-Based Civic Education Programs," paper presented at the Annual Meeting of the American Political Science Association, Boston, 2002. Richard Battistoni outlines multiple conceptions of civic engagement in *Civic Engagement Across the Curriculum* (Providence: Campus Compact, 2002).

48. Keeter et al., *The Civic and Political Health of the Nation: A Generational Portrait* (College Park, Maryland: Center for Information and Research on Civic Learning and Engagement, 2002). See also Scott Keeter et al., *A Guide to the Index of Civic and Political Engagement* (College Park, Maryland: Center for Information and Research on Civic Learning and Engagement, 2003).

49. Milbrey McLaughlin et al., *Urban Sanctuaries: Neighborhood Organizations in the Lives and Futures of Inner-City Youth* (San Francisco: Jossey-Bass, 1994), p. 4.

See also Milbrey McLaughlin, *Community Counts: How Youth Organizations Matter for Youth Development* (Washington, D.C.: Public Education Network, 2000).

50. See, for example, William Galston, "Political Knowledge, Political Engagement, and Civic Education," *Annual Review of Political Science 4* (2001): 217–234. The HERI survey conducted by UCLA has been tracking this data for incoming college students; see Linda Sax et al., *The American Freshman: National Norms for Fall 2003* (Los Angeles: Higher Education Research Institute, UCLA Graduate School of Education and Information Studies, 2003).

51. Sylvia Hurtado et al., *The American Freshman: National Norms for Fall 2005* (Los Angeles: Higher Education Research Institute, UCLA Graduate School of Education and Information Studies, 2005). The most impressive resource for data on youth civic engagement of all kinds, including volunteering, can be found on the CIRCLE Web site: www.civicyouth.org.

52. See, for example, Harry C. Boyte, *Everyday Politics: Reconnecting Citizens and Public Life* (Philadelphia: University of Pennsylvania, 2004).

53. John McKnight, *The Careless Society: Community and Its Counterfeits* (New York: Basic Books, 1995).

54. Harry C. Boyte, "Community Service and Civic Education," *Phi Delta Kappan* (June 1991): 765–767, p. 766.

55. See, for example, William Galston, "Political Knowledge, Political Engagement, and Civic Education," *Annual Review of Political Science 4* (2001): 217–234.

56. David Mathews, "Reviewing and Previewing Civics," in *Educating the Democratic Mind*, ed. Walter Parker (Albany: SUNY Press, 1996), p. 271.

57. Sarah Long, *The New Student Politics: The Wingspread Statement on Student Civic Engagement* (Providence: Campus Compact, 2002). For a longer discussion of the alternative politics on college campuses, see Nicholas V. Longo and Ross P. Meyer, "College Students and Politics: A Literature Review," CIRCLE Working Paper 46 (College Park, Maryland: Center for Information and Research on Civic Learning and Engagement, May 2006).

58. Quoted from E. J. Dionne, "Effective Citizenship and the Spirit of Our Time," paper prepared for the Surdna Foundation, New York, 2000, p. 20.

59. Harry C. Boyte, "Necessity of Politics," *Journal of Public Affairs 7* (2004): 75–85, p. 85.

60. I directed Raise Your Voice for Campus Compact from 2002 to 2004, then helped to create a manual for student-organizing efforts on campuses. See Richard Cone, Abby Kiesa, and Nicholas V. Longo, eds, *Raise Your Voice: A Student Guide to Making Positive Social Change* (Providence: Campus Compact, 2006).

61. Theodore Sizer, *The Red Pencil: Convictions from Experience in Education* (New Haven: Yale University Press, 2004), p. 24.

62. Quoted in Ira Harkavy and Marty Blank, "Community Schools: A Vision of Learning That Goes Beyond Testing," *Education Week*, April 17, 2002, p. 52.

63. Harry C. Boyte, "A Different Kind of Politics: John Dewey and the Meaning of Citizenship in the 21st Century," speech presented at the University of Michigan, November 1, 2002.

Chapter Two

Epigraph from William Kilpatrick, "Introduction: The Underlying Philosophy of Cooperative Activities for Community Improvement," in Paul Hanna, *Youth Serves the Community* (New York: D. Appleton-Century Company, 1936), p. 7.

1. John Dewey, "The School as Social Centre," *The Middle Works, 1899–1924,* vol. 2 (Carbondale: Southern Illinois University Press, 1976/1902), pp. 92–93.

2. The implications for Dewey's speech for community and adult education are examined by Jerome Stein in "John Dewey and Adult Education" (PhD diss., University of Minnesota, 1992). Others have discussed the importance of this speech, including Lee Benson and Ira Harkavy, "Integrating the American System of Higher, Secondary, and Primary Education to Develop Civic Responsibility," in *Civic Responsibility and Higher Education,* ed. Thomas Ehrlich (Phoenix: American Council on Education., 2000); Harry C. Boyte, "A Different Kind of Politics: John Dewey and the Meaning of Citizenship in the 21st Century," speech presented at the University of Michigan, November 1, 2002; and William Denton, "Community Education: On the Forefront of Educational Reform(?) Part I: The Evolution of the Movement," *Community Education Journal 26* (1998): 28–34.

3. John Dewey, "The School as Social Centre," *The Middle Works, 1899–1924,* vol. 2 (Carbondale: Southern Illinois University Press, 1976/1902), pp. 90–91.

4. Ira Harkavy and John Puckett, "Lessons from Hull House for the Contemporary Urban University," *Social Science Review* (September 1994): 299–321, esp. 311-312.

5. Discussions of these developments in community-based education are found in William Denton, "Community Education: On the Forefront of Educational Reform(?) Part I: The Evolution of the Movement," *Community Education Journal 26* (1998): 28–34; William Denton, "Community Education: On the Forefront of Educational Reform(?) Part II: Institutionalizing the Movement," *Community Education Journal 27* (1999): 28–36; Lawrence Cremin, *The Metropolitan Experience 1876–1980* (New York: Harper & Row, 1988); and Keith Morton and John Saltmarsh, "Addams, Day and Dewey: The Emergence of Community Service in American Culture," *Michigan Journal of Community Service-Learning 4* (1997): 137–149.

6. Ellen Lagemann, ed., *Jane Addams on Education* (New Brunswick: Transaction Publishers, 1994), p. xiv.

7. For a review of some of these, see William Denton, "Community Education: On the Forefront of Educational Reform(?) Part I: The Evolution of the Movement," *Community Education Journal 26* (1998): 28–34; and Paul DeLargy, "Public Schools and Community Education," in *Handbook of Adult and Continuing Education,* eds. Sharan Merriam and Phyllis Cunningham (San Francisco: Jossey-Bass, 1989).

8. See Lawrence Cremin, *The Metropolitan Experience 1876–1980* (New York: Harper and Row, 1988); Robert Westbrook, *John Dewey and American Democracy* (Ithaca: Cornell University Press, 1991); and Diane Ravitch, *Left Back: A Century of Battles over School Reform* (New York: Simon and Schuster, 2000).

9. Joseph Hart, *Education in the Humane Community* (New York: Harper and Brothers, 1951).

10. Joseph Hart, *The Discovery of Intelligence* (New York: The Century Company, 1924), pp. 382–383.

11. Joseph Hart, *The Discovery of Intelligence* (New York: The Century Company, 1924), p. 424.

12. These movements are well chronicled in William Denton's history of community education. See William Denton, "Community Education: On the Forefront of Educational Reform(?) Part I: The Evolution of the Movement," *Community Education Journal 26* (1998): 28–34 and William Denton, "Community Education: On the Forefront of Educational Reform(?) Part II: Institutionalizing the Movement," *Community Education Journal 27* (1999): 28–36.

13. William Denton, "Community Education: On the Forefront of Educational Reform(?) Part I: The Evolution of the Movement," *Community Education Journal 26* (1998): 28–34.

14. Quoted in Kevin Mattson, *Creating a Democratic Public: The Struggle for Urban Participatory Democracy During the Progressive Era* (University Park: The Pennsylvania State University Press, 1998), p. 49. This section draws on Mattson's excellent research on the social centers.

15. Kevin Mattson, *Creating a Democratic Public: The Struggle for Urban Participatory Democracy During the Progressive Era* (University Park: The Pennsylvania State University Press, 1998), p. 59.

16. Quoted in Kevin Mattson, *Creating a Democratic Public: The Struggle for Urban Participatory Democracy During the Progressive Era* (University Park: The Pennsylvania State University Press, 1998), p. 54.

17. Again, for good overviews of social centers, see William Denton, "Community Education: On the Forefront of Educational Reform(?) Part I: The Evolution of the Movement," *Community Education Journal 26* (1998): 28–34, and Kevin Mattson, *Creating a Democratic Public: The Struggle for Urban Participatory Democracy During the Progressive Era* (University Park: The Pennsylvania State University Press, 1998).

18. Quoted in Kevin Mattson, *Creating a Democratic Public: The Struggle for Urban Participatory Democracy During the Progressive Era* (University Park: The Pennsylvania State University Press, 1998), p. 13.

19. Quoted in Kevin Mattson, *Creating a Democratic Public: The Struggle for Urban Participatory Democracy During the Progressive Era* (University Park: The Pennsylvania State University Press, 1998), p. 13.

20. Quoted in Kevin Mattson, *Creating a Democratic Public: The Struggle for Urban Participatory Democracy During the Progressive Era* (University Park: The Pennsylvania State University Press, 1998), p. 13.

21. Jerome Stein, "John Dewey and Adult Education" (PhD diss., University of Minnesota, 1992), p. 64.

22. William Denton, "Community Education: On the Forefront of Educational Reform(?) Part I: The Evolution of the Movement," *Community Education Journal 26* (1998): 28–34.

23. Robert Fisher, *Let the People Decide: Neighborhood Organizing in America* (New York: Twayne Publishers, 1994).

24. Nelson B. Henry, *The Fifty-second Yearbook of the National Society for the Study of Education: Part II the Community School* (Chicago: University of Chicago Press, 1953).

25. Paul DeLargy, "Public Schools and Community Education," in *Handbook of Adult and Continuing Education*, eds. Sharan Merriam and Phyllis Cunningham (San Francisco: Jossey-Bass, 1989).

26. Henry Barnard, *Report of the Conditions and Improvements of the Public Schools of Rhode Island* (Providence: B. Cranston and Co., 1845), p. 70.

27. Ibid., p. 78.

28. John Dewey and Evelyn Dewey, *Schools of Tomorrow* (Honolulu: University Press of the Pacific, 2003/1915), p. 228.

29. John Dewey and Evelyn Dewey, *Schools of Tomorrow* (Honolulu: University Press of the Pacific, 2003/1915), p. 185.

30. *The Civic Mission of Schools* (New York: Carnegie Corporation and Center for Information and Research on Civic Learning and Engagement, 2003).

31. John Dewey and Evelyn Dewey, *Schools of Tomorrow* (Honolulu: University Press of the Pacific, 2003/1915), p. 208.

32. See Charlene Haddock Seigfried, *Pragmatism and Feminism: Reweaving the Social Fabric* (Chicago: University of Chicago Press, 1996).

33. Elsie Clapp, *Community Schools in Action* (New York: Viking Press, 1939), Elsie Clapp, *The Use of Resources in Education* (New York: Harper & Brothers, 1952).

34. Elsie Clapp, *Community Schools in Action* (New York: Viking Press, 1939), p. 3.

35. Ibid., p. 89.

36. Ibid., pp. 355–356.

37. Quoted in Jerome Stein, "John Dewey and Adult Education" (PhD diss., University of Minnesota, 1992), p. 103.

38. Samuel Everett, ed., *The Community School* (New York: D. Appleton-Century Company, 1938), pp. 437–438.

39. Vito Perrone helped reintroduce Covello to contemporary educators in *Teacher with a Heart: Reflections on Leonard Covello and Community* (New York: Teachers College Press, 1998). See also Michael Johanek and John Puckett, *Education as if Citizens Mattered: Leonard Covello and the Idea of Community Schools* (Philadelphia: Temple University Press, 2006).

40. Leonard Covello, "The School as the Center of Community Life in an Immigrant Area," in *The Community School*, ed. Samuel Everett (New York: D. Appleton-Century Company, 1938), p. 130.

41. Leonard Covello, *The Heart Is the Teacher* (New York: McGraw-Hill, 1958), p. 210.

42. Ibid., pp. 205–206.

43. Ibid., p. 217.

44. Ibid., pp. 217–218.

45. For a fuller description of the community schools, see Larry Decker, *Foundation of Community Education* (Midland, Michigan: Pendell Publishing, 1972); Paul DeLargy, "Public Schools and Community Education," in *Handbook*

of Adult and Continuing Education, eds. Sharan Merriam and Phyllis Cunningham (San Francisco: Jossey-Bass, 1989); and William Denton, "Community Education: On the Forefront of Educational Reform(?) Part II: Institutionalizing the Movement," *Community Education Journal 27* (1999): 28–36.

46. Marty Blank, "How Community Schools Make a Difference," *Education Leadership 61* (May 2004): 62–65, esp. 62.

47. Marty Blank et al., *Making the Difference: Research and Practice in Community Schools* (Washington, D.C.: Coalition for Community Schools, Institute for Educational Leadership, 2003).

48. Thomas Sergiovanni, *Building Community in Schools* (San Francisco: Jossey-Bass, 1994) and Deborah Meier, *The Power of Their Ideas: Lessons for America from a Small School in Harlem* (Boston: Beacon Press, 1995).

49. See Joy Dryfoos, "The Role of the School in Children's Out-of-School Time," *The Future of Children 9,* no. 2 (Fall 1999): 117–134.

50. *Building a Community School* (New York: The Children's Aid Society, 2001), p. 53.

51. Lisbeth Schorr, *Common Purpose: Strengthening Families and Neighborhoods to Rebuild America* (New York: Anchor Books, 1997).

52. Beacons are examined in *Beacons: A Union of Youth and Community Development* (Washington, D.C.: International Youth Foundation, 1997); Carmen Sirianni, Melissa Bass, and Lewis Friedland, *Youth Leadership for Civic Renewal: Mapping Networks, Catalyzing Action* (Philadelphia: Pew Charitable Trusts Public Policy Program, 2000); and Joy Dryfoos, "The Role of the School in Children's Out-of-School Time," *The Future of Children 9,* no. 2 (Fall 1999): 117–134.

53. For a good overview of the impact of John Dewey on higher education, see Lee Benson and Ira Harkavy, "Integrating the American System of Higher, Secondary, and Primary Education to Develop Civic Responsibility," in *Civic Responsibility and Higher Education,* ed. Thomas Ehrlich (Phoenix: American Council on Education, 2000). See also Benson et al., *Dewey's Dreams* (Philadelphia: Temple University Press, 2007).

54. Ernest Boyer, *Selected Speeches 1979–1995* (Princeton: The Carnegie Foundation for the Advancement of Teaching, 1997), p. 92.

55. Ira Harkavy, especially, has written and spoken extensively on the democratic tradition of higher education. See also Ernest Boyer, *Scholarship Reconsidered: Priorities of the Professoriate* (Princeton: The Carnegie Foundation for the Advancement of Teaching, 1990), and Ernest Boyer, "Creating the New American College," *The Chronicle of Higher Education* (March 9, 1994): A48.

56. Quoted in Lee Benson and Ira Harkavy, "Integrating the American System of Higher, Secondary, and Primary Education to Develop Civic Responsibility," in *Civic Responsibility and Higher Education,* ed. Thomas Ehrlich (Phoenix: American Council on Education., 2000), p. 179.

57. Quoted in Ernest Boyer, *Scholarship Reconsidered: Priorities of the Professoriate* (Princeton: The Carnegie Foundation for the Advancement of Teaching, 1990), p. 5.

58. See Eugene Rice, *Making a Place for the New America Scholar* (Washington, D.C.: American Association of Higher Education, 1996); Ernest Boyer, *Scholarship*

Reconsidered: Priorities of the Professoriate (Princeton: The Carnegie Foundation for the Advancement of Teaching, 1990); and Ernest Boyer, "Creating the New American College," *The Chronicle of Higher Education* (March 9, 1994): A48.

59. For a discussion of the challenges to a civic mission, see Harry C. Boyte and Nan Kari, "Renewing the Democratic Spirit in American Colleges and Universities: Higher Education as Public Work," in *Civic Responsibility and Higher Education*, ed. Thomas Erlich (Phoenix: American Council on Education, 2000); and William Sullivan, "Institutional Identity and Social Responsibility in Higher Education," in *Civic Responsibility and Higher Education*, ed. Thomas Erlich (Phoenix: American Council on Education, 2000).

60. David Maurrasse, *Beyond the Campus: How Colleges and Universities Form Partnerships with Their Communities* (New York: Routledge, 2001), p. 28.

61. Ernest Boyer, "Creating the New American College," *The Chronicle of Higher Education* (March 9, 1994): A48.

62. Donald Schön, *The Reflective Practitioner: How Professionals Think in Action* (New York: Basic Books, 1983).

63. Nicholas V. Longo et al., *Colleges with a Conscience* (New York: Random House, 2005).

64. Lee Benson, and Ira Harkavy, "Leading the Way to Meaningful Partnerships," *Principal Leadership* (September 2001): 54–58, esp. 54.

65. For a description of the efforts at the Center for Community Partnerships, see Ira Harkavy and Nicholas V. Longo, "Problem-Solving with Local Communities: Using University-Community-School Partnerships and Place-Based Education to Help Revitalize Urban America," *Democracy and Education 16*, no. 2 (2006): 16–23.

66. Thomas Ehrlich and Elizabeth Hollander, *The Presidents' Declaration on the Civic Responsibility of Higher Education* (Providence: Campus Compact, 1999).

67. *Oklahoma Students' Civic Resolution* (Providence: Campus Compact, 2003). Retrieved June 21, 2006, from www.actionforchange.org/getinformed/student_ink.

68. Although access to higher education continues to be an issue of major public concern, in October 2004, 66.7 percent of high school graduates from the class of 2004 were enrolled in colleges or universities, according to the U.S. Department of Labor's Bureau of Labor Statistics. The U.S. Department of Education reports that college enrollment hit a record level of 17.1 million in fall 2004, and enrollment is expected to increase by an additional 14 percent between 2004 and 2014. Further, one in three of the more than 13 million undergraduates attends a two-year educational institution according to U.S. Census in 2003.

Chapter Three

Epigraph from John Dewey quoted in *One Hundred Years at Hull-House*, eds. Mary L. Bryan and Allen Davis (Bloomington: Indiana University Press, 1990/1930), p. 191.

1. Ellen Lagemann, ed., *Jane Addams on Education* (New Brunswick: Transaction Publishers, 1994), p. xv.

2. Jane Addams, "The Humanizing Tendency of Industrial Education," in *Jane Addams on Education*, ed. Ellen Lagemann (New York: Teacher's College Press, 1994/1904), p. 120.

3. Jane Addams, *Twenty Years at Hull House* (New York: Penguin Books, 1998/1910), p. 275.

4. Jane Addams, *Twenty Years at Hull House* (New York: Penguin Books, 1998/1910), p. 286.

5. Lawrence Cremin, *The Metropolitan Experience 1876–1980* (New York: Harper and Row, 1988), p. 177.

6. Ellen Lagemann, ed., *Jane Addams on Education* (New Brunswick: Transaction Publishers, 1994), pp. xiv–xv.

7. See Allen Davis, *Spearheads for Reform: The Social Settlements and the Progressive Movement 1890–1914* (New Brunswick: Rutgers University Press, 1991) and Daniel Levine, *Jane Addams and the Liberal Tradition* (Westport, Connecticut: Greenwood, 1971).

8. Jane Addams, *Twenty Years at Hull House* (New York: Penguin Books, 1998/1910).

9. Jean Bethke Elshtain, *Jane Addams and the Dream of American Democracy* (New York: Basic Books, 2002) and Jean Bethke Elshtain, ed., *The Jane Addams Reader* (New York: Basic Books, 2002). In previous decades, Addams's, writing was published by Ellen Lagemann, ed., *Jane Addams on Education* (New Brunswick: Transaction Publishers, 1994) and Christopher Lasch, ed., *The Social Thought of Jane Addams* (New York: Bobbs-Merrill, 1965). See also Louise Knight, *Citizen: Jane Addams and the Struggle for Democracy* (Chicago: University of Chicago Press, 2005); Victoria Brown, *The Education of Jane Addams* (Philadelphia: University of Pennsylvania Press, 2004); and Katherine Joslin, *Jane Addams: A Writer's Life* (Urbana: University of Illinois Press, 2004).

10. Jane Addams, *The Spirit of Youth and the City Streets* (Chicago: University of Illinois Press, 1972/1909), and Jane Addams, *The Long Road of Woman's Memory* (Chicago: University of Illinois Press, 2002/1916).

11. Jane Addams has been invoked in several important pieces on the history of service-learning and civic education. See Harry C. Boyte and Nan Kari, *Building America: The Democratic Promise of Public Work* (Philadelphia: Temple University Press, 1996); Ira Harkavy and John Puckett, "Lessons from Hull House for the Contemporary Urban University," *Social Science Review* (September 1994): 299–321; and Keith Morton and John Saltmarsh, "Addams, Day and Dewey: The Emergence of Community Service in American Culture," *Michigan Journal of Community Service-Learning 4* (1997): 137–149. See also Gary Daynes and Nicholas V. Longo, "Jane Addams and the Origins of Service-Learning Practice in the United States," *Michigan Journal of Community Service-Learning 11* (Fall 2004): 5–13.

12. This argument was developed further in an article I wrote with Gary Daynes. See Gary Daynes and Nicholas V. Longo, "Jane Addams and the Origins of Service-Learning Practice in the United States," *Michigan Journal of Community Service-Learning 11* (Fall 2004): 5–13.

13. Jane Addams, "The Second Twenty Years at Hull House," in *The Social Thought of Jane Addams*, ed. Christopher Lasch (New York: Bobbs-Merrill, 1965), p. 216.

14. Jane Addams, "The Second Twenty Years at Hull House," in *The Social Thought of Jane Addams*, ed. Christopher Lasch (New York: Bobbs-Merrill, 1965), p. 216.

15. Mary Lynn Bryan and Allen Davis, *One Hundred Years at Hull-House* (Bloomington: Indiana University Press, 1990).

16. Allen Davis, *Spearheads for Reform: The Social Settlements and the Progressive Movement 1890–1914* (New Brunswick: Rutgers University Press, 1991).

17. Jane Addams, *Twenty Years at Hull House* (New York: Penguin Books, 1998/1910); Mary Lynn Bryan and Allen Davis, *One Hundred Years at Hull-House* (Bloomington: Indiana University Press, 1990); and Allen Davis, *American Heroine: The Life and Legend of Jane Addams* (New York: Oxford University Press, 1973).

18. Quoted in Allen Davis, *American Heroine: The Life and Legend of Jane Addams* (New York: Oxford University Press, 1973), p. 96.

19. Jane Addams, "A Function of the Social Settlement," in *The Social Thought of Jane Addams*, ed. Christopher Lasch (New York: Bobbs-Merrill, 1965/1899).

20. Jane Addams, *Democracy and Social Ethics* (Chicago: University of Illinois Press, 2002/1902), p. 118. Harry Boyte points out the civic populist dimensions of Jane Addams's critique of the "expert driven" reformers in Harry C. Boyte, "The Civic Renewal Movement in the U.S.: On Silences and Civic Muscle, or Why Social Capital is a Useful But Insufficient Concept," speech presented at the Havens Center, University of Wisconsin–Madison, April 10, 2001.

21. *Hull House Maps and Papers* (New York: Thomas Crowell, 1895).

22. Lawrence Cremin, *The Metropolitan Experience 1876–1980* (New York: Harper and Row, 1988), p. 175.

23. This description comes from several sources. See Gioia Diliberto, *A Useful Woman: The Early Life of Jane Addams* (New York: Scribner, 1999); Mary Lynn Bryan and Allen Davis, *One Hundred Years at Hull-House* (Bloomington: Indiana University Press, 1990); and Allen Davis, *American Heroine: The Life and Legend of Jane Addams* (New York: Oxford University Press, 1973).

24. Jane Addams, *Twenty Years at Hull House* (New York: Penguin Books, 1998/1910), p. 61.

25. Quoted in Gioia Diliberto, *A Useful Woman: The Early Life of Jane Addams* (New York: Scribner, 1999), p. 131.

26. Jane Addams, *Twenty Years at Hull House* (New York: Penguin Books, 1998/1910), p. 61.

27. Jane Addams, "A Function of the Social Settlement," in *The Social Thought of Jane Addams*, ed. Christopher Lasch (New York: Bobbs-Merrill, 1965/1899), p. 187.

28. Jane Addams, *Twenty Years at Hull House* (New York: Penguin Books, 1998/1910), p. 83.

29. Quoted in Allen Davis, *American Heroine: The Life and Legend of Jane Addams* (New York: Oxford University Press, 1973), p. 69.

30. These stories come from Allen Davis, *American Heroine: The Life and Legend of Jane Addams* (New York: Oxford University Press, 1973) and Jean Bethke Elshtain, *Jane Addams and the Dream of American Democracy* (New York: Basic Books, 2002).

31. Quoted in Jean Bethke Elshtain, *Jane Addams and the Dream of American Democracy* (New York: Basic Books, 2002), p. 93.

32. See Jean Bethke Elshtain, ed., *The Jane Addams Reader* (New York: Basic Books, 2002) and Jean Bethke Elshtain, *Jane Addams and the Dream of American Democracy* (New York: Basic Books, 2002).

33. Quoted in Allen Davis, *American Heroine: The Life and Legend of Jane Addams* (New York: Oxford University Press, 1973), p. 68.

34. Quoted in Ellen Lagemann, ed., *Jane Addams on Education* (New Brunswick: Transaction Publishers, 1994), p. 23.

35. Jane Addams, "The Subtle Problem of Charity," in *The Jane Addams Reader*, ed. Jean Bethke Elshtain (New York: Basic Books, 1899/2002), p. 62.

36. Gary Daynes and I made this argument in Gary Daynes and Nicholas V. Longo, "Jane Addams and the Origins of Service-Learning Practice in the United States," *Michigan Journal of Community Service-Learning 11* (Fall 2004): 5–13.

37. Quoted in Jean Bethke Elshtain, *Jane Addams and the Dream of American Democracy* (New York: Basic Books, 2002), p. 187.

38. Jane Addams, *Twenty Years at Hull House* (New York: Penguin Books, 1998/1910), p. 280.

39. Mary Lynn Bryan and Allen Davis, *One Hundred Years at Hull-House* (Bloomington: Indiana University Press, 1990). An excellent discussion of the funding for Hull House comes from Kathryn K. Sklar, "Who Funded Hull House?" in *Lady Bountiful Revisited: Women, Philanthropy, and Power*, ed. Kathleen McCarthy (New Brunswick: Rutgers University Press, 1990).

40. Florence Kelley "Hull House," *New England Magazine 18*, no. 5 (July, 1898): 550-566, p. 550.

41. Quoted in Mary Lynn Bryan and Allen Davis, *One Hundred Years at Hull-House* (Bloomington: Indiana University Press, 1990), p. 112.

42. See Lawrence Cremin, *The Metropolitan Experience 1876–1980* (New York: Harper and Row, 1988).

43. John Dewey and Evelyn Dewey, *Schools of Tomorrow* (Honolulu: University Press of the Pacific, 2003/1915), pp. 205–206.

44. John Dewey, letter from John Dewey to Jane Addams (January 27, 1892), Rockford College Archives.

45. Quoted in Allen Davis, *American Heroine: The Life and Legend of Jane Addams* (New York: Oxford University Press, 1973), p. 97. For a discussion of the relationship between John Dewey and Jane Addams, see also Louis Menand, *The Metaphysical Club: A Story of Ideas in America* (New York: Farrar, Straus and Giroux, 2001) and Charlene Haddock Seigfried, "Socializing Democracy: Jane Addams and John Dewey," *Philosophy of the Social Sciences 29*, no. 2 (1999): 207–230.

46. Allen Davis, *Spearheads for Reform: The Social Settlements and the Progressive Movement 1890–1914* (New Brunswick: Rutgers University Press, 1991).

47. Christopher Lasch, ed., *The Social Thought of Jane Addams* (New York: Bobbs-Merrill, 1965), p. 176.

48. This argument is made by Charlene Haddock Seigfried in *Pragmatism and Feminism: Reweaving the Social Fabric* (Chicago: University of Chicago Press, 1996).

49. Lawrence Cremin, *The Metropolitan Experience 1876–1980* (New York: Harper and Row, 1988), p. 179.

50. John Dewey, "The School as Social Centre," *The Middle Works, 1899–1924*, vol. 2 (Carbondale: Southern Illinois University Press, 1976/1902); John Dewey, *Democracy and Education* (New York: Macmillan, 1916); and John Dewey, *The Public and Its Problems* (New York: Holt, 1927).

51. Jerome Stein, "John Dewey and Adult Education" (PhD diss., University of Minnesota, 1992), p. 55.

52. John Dewey and Evelyn Dewey, *Schools of Tomorrow* (Honolulu: University Press of the Pacific, 2003/1915).

53. Charlene Haddock Seigfried, "Socializing Democracy: Jane Addams and John Dewey," *Philosophy of the Social Sciences 29*, no. 2 (1999): 207–230, esp. 213. See also Gary Daynes and Nicholas V. Longo, "Jane Addams and the Origins of Service-Learning Practice in the United States," *Michigan Journal of Community Service-Learning 11* (Fall 2004): 5–13.

54. Jerome Stein persuasively argues that Dewey's focus actually shifted from the schools to the community in his later writings; see Jerome Stein, "John Dewey and Adult Education" (PhD diss., University of Minnesota, 1992).

55. Lawrence Cremin, *The Metropolitan Experience 1876–1980* (New York: Harper and Row, 1988), p. 179.

56. Jane Addams, *Democracy and Social Ethics* (Chicago: University of Illinois Press, 2002/1902), p. 83.

57. Jane Addams "The Objective Value of a Social Settlement," in *The Social Thought of Jane Addams*, Christopher Lasch, ed. (New York: Bobbs-Merrill, 1892/1965), p. 54.

58. Jane Addams, "Jane Addams's Own Story of Her Work: Fifteen Years at Hull House," in *The Ladies' Home Journal* (March 2006): 13–14, esp. 14.

59. Allen Davis, *American Heroine: The Life and Legend of Jane Addams* (New York: Oxford University Press, 1973).

60. Jane Addams, "A Function of the Social Settlement," in *The Social Thought of Jane Addams*, ed. Christopher Lasch (New York: Bobbs-Merrill, 1965/1899), p. 199.

61. Ibid., p. 187.

62. Jane Addams, "A Function of the Social Settlement," in *The Social Thought of Jane Addams*, ed. Christopher Lasch (New York: Bobbs-Merrill, 1965/1899), p. 196. This argument is made in Gary Daynes and Nicholas V. Longo, "Jane Addams and the Origins of Service-Learning Practice in the United States," *Michigan Journal of Community Service-Learning 11* (Fall 2004): 5–13.

63. Ira Harkavy and John Puckett, "Lessons from Hull House for the Contemporary Urban University," *Social Science Review* (September 1994): 299–321, esp. 309.

64. Ibid., p. 312.

65. Jane Addams, *Democracy and Social Ethics* (Chicago: University of Illinois Press, 2002/1902), p. 80.

66. Harry Boyte and Nan Kari, *Building America: The Democratic Promise of Public Work* (Philadelphia: Temple University Press, 1996), p. 87.

67. Jane Addams, "The Subtle Problem of Charity," in *The Jane Addams Reader*, ed. Jean Bethke Elshtain (New York: Basic Books, 1899/2002).

68. Jane Addams, "A Function of the Social Settlement," in *The Social Thought of Jane Addams*, ed. Christopher Lasch (New York: Bobbs-Merrill, 1965/1899), p. 193.

69. Jane Addams, "The Humanizing Tendency of Industrial Education," in *Jane Addams on Education*, ed. Ellen Lagemann (New York: Teacher's College Press, 1994/1904), p. 277.

70. Paulo Freire, *Pedagogy of the Oppressed* (New York: Continuum, 2000/1970).

71. Jane Addams, "Widening the Circle of Enlightenment: Hull House and Adult Education," in *Jane Addams on Education*, ed. Ellen Lagemann (New York: Teacher's College Press, 1994/1930), p. 206.

72. Jane Addams, *Democracy and Social Ethics* (Chicago: University of Illinois Press, 2002/1902), p. 220.

73. See Jane Addams, "First Report of a Labor Museum at Hull House," *Unity* (March 13, 1902): 20–23, Jessie Luther, "The Labor Museum at Hull House," *The Commons 70* (May 1902): 1–17, Jane Addams, *Twenty Years at Hull House* (New York: Penguin Books, 1998/1910), Jane Addams, "The Hull House Labor Museum," *Chatauquan 38* (September 1903): 60–61.

74. Jane Addams, "Hull House and Its Neighbors," *Charities 12* (May 7, 1904): 450–451, esp. 451.

75. Jane Addams, "The Hull House Labor Museum," *Chatauquan 38* (September 1903): 60–61. Mary Lynn Bryan and Allen Davis, *One Hundred Years at Hull-House* (Bloomington: Indiana University Press, 1990).

76. Marion Washburne, "A Labor Museum," *The Craftsman 6*, no. 6 (September 1904): 570–579.

77. Quoted in Jean Bethke Elshtain, *Jane Addams and the Dream of American Democracy* (New York: Basic Books, 2002), p. 145.

78. Jane Addams, "Hull House and Its Neighbors," *Charities 12* (May 7, 1904): 450–451, esp. 451.

79. Jane Addams, *American Education* (March 1906), p. 416.

80. Marion Washburne, "A Labor Museum," *The Craftsman 6*, no. 6 (September 1904): 570–579, esp. 571.

81. Jane Addams, *Twenty Years at Hull House* (New York: Penguin Books, 1998/1910), p. 159.

82. Mary Lynn Bryan and Allen Davis, *One Hundred Years at Hull-House* (Bloomington: Indiana University Press, 1990).

83. Quoted in Jean Bethke Elshtain, *Jane Addams and the Dream of American Democracy* (New York: Basic Books, 2002), p. 154.

Chapter Four

Epigraph from Myles Horton with Judith Kohl and Herbert Kohl, *The Long Haul: An Autobiography* (New York: Teacher's College Press, 1998), p. 49.

1. Myles Horton, "Letter to Dr. Alice Hamilton" (Highlander Papers: Box 96, March 5, 1969).

2. Ibid.

3. Myles Horton with Judith Kohl and Herbert Kohl, *The Long Haul: An Autobiography* (New York: Teacher's College Press, 1998), p. 48. Myles Horton, "Interview with Frank Adams" (Highlander Papers, n.d.).

4. Myles Horton with Judith Kohl and Herbert Kohl, *The Long Haul: An Autobiography* (New York: Teacher's College Press, 1998), pp. 48–49.

5. Frank Adams, *Unearthing Seeds of Fire: The Idea of Highlander* (Winston-Salem, North Carolina: John F. Blair, 1975).

6. See Myles Horton, "Interview with Frank Adams" (Highlander Papers, n.d.).

7. Aimee Horton, *The Highlander Folk School: A History of Its Major Programs, 1932-1961* (Brooklyn: Carlson Publishing, 1989), p. 25.

8. Quoted in Frank Adams, *Unearthing Seeds of Fire: The Idea of Highlander* (Winston-Salem, North Carolina: John F. Blair, 1975), p. 24.

9. John Glen, *Highlander: No Ordinary School* (Knoxville: The University of Tennessee Press, 1996).

10. Aimee Horton, *The Highlander Folk School: A History of its Major Programs, 1932–1961* (Brooklyn: Carlson Publishing, 1989). In another interesting connection between Addams and Horton, Aimee Horton, Myles's second wife, attended Rockford College, Addams's alma matter; like Addams, she realized she wanted to "do something" to impact the world while at Rockford, according to interviews by Sue Himplemann and Norma Nerstrom in 1999.

11. Frank Adams, *Unearthing Seeds of Fire: The Idea of Highlander* (Winston-Salem, North Carolina: John F. Blair, 1975).

12. Myles Horton with Judith Kohl and Herbert Kohl, *The Long Haul: An Autobiography* (New York: Teacher's College Press, 1998), and Cynthia Stokes Brown, ed., *Ready from Within: Septima Clark and the Civil Rights Movement* (Trenton, New Jersey: Africa World Press, 1990).

13. Myles Horton and Paulo Freire, *We Make the Road by Walking: Conversations on Education and Social Change* (Philadelphia: Temple University Press, 1990).

14. Dale Jacobs, *The Myles Horton Reader: Education for Social Change* (Knoxville: The University of Tennessee Press, 2003).

15. Lawrence Cremin, *The Metropolitan Experience 1876–1980* (New York: Harper and Row, 1988).

16. Steven Borish, *The Land of the Living: The Danish Folk High Schools and Denmark's Non-Violent Path to Modernization* (Nevada City, California: Blue Dolphin Publishing, 1991).

17. John Dewey, Letter to Highlander Folk School, September 27, 1933 (Highlander Papers).

18. John Dewey, *Nashville Banner*, letter to the editor, October 12, 1940, and Aimee Horton, *The Highlander Folk School: A History of its Major Programs, 1932–1961* (Brooklyn: Carlson Publishing, 1989), p. 138.

19. Dale Jacobs, *The Myles Horton Reader: Education for Social Change* (Knoxville: The University of Tennessee Press, 2003), p. xxvii.

20. These descriptions, along with the story of the closing and reopening of Highlander, appear in Cynthia Stokes Brown, ed., *Ready from Within: Septima Clark and the Civil Rights Movement* (Trenton, New Jersey: Africa World Press, 1990); C. Alvin Hughes, "A New Agenda for the South: The Role and Influence of the Highlander Folk School, 1953–1961," *Phylon 46*, no. 3 (September 1985): 242–250; Frank Adams, *Unearthing Seeds of Fire: The Idea of Highlander* (Winston-Salem, North Carolina: John F. Blair, 1975); John Glen, *Highlander: No Ordinary School* (Knoxville: The University of Tennessee Press, 1996); and Aimee Horton, *The Highlander Folk School: A History of Its Major Programs, 1932–1961* (Brooklyn: Carlson Publishing, 1989).

21. Myles Horton with Judith Kohl and Herbert Kohl, *The Long Haul: An Autobiography* (New York: Teacher's College Press, 1998), p. 149.

22. Quoted from Frank Adams, *Unearthing Seeds of Fire: The Idea of Highlander* (Winston-Salem, North Carolina: John F. Blair, 1975), p. 122.

23. Myles Horton with Judith Kohl and Herbert Kohl, *The Long Haul: An Autobiography* (New York: Teacher's College Press, 1998), p. 68.

24. C. Alvin Hughes, "A New Agenda for the South: The Role and Influence of the Highlander Folk School, 1953-1961," *Phylon 46*, no. 3 (September 1985): 242–250.

25. Quoted in C. Alvin Hughes, "A New Agenda for the South: The Role and Influence of the Highlander Folk School, 1953–1961," *Phylon 46*, no. 3 (September 1985): 242–250, esp. 243.

26. Some of these criticisms of Highlander can be found in Aldon Morris, "Introduction: Education for Liberation," *Social Policy 21*, no. 3 (Winter 1991): 2–6.

27. Myles Horton, "An Interview with Myles Horton: It's a Miracle—I Still Don't Believe It," *Phi Delta Kappan* (May 1966): 490–497, esp. 490.

28. Myles Horton with Judith Kohl and Herbert Kohl, *The Long Haul: An Autobiography* (New York: Teacher's College Press, 1998), p. 157.

29. Myles Horton, "An Interview with Myles Horton: It's a Miracle—I Still Don't Believe It," *Phi Delta Kappan* (May 1966): 490–497.

30. See especially Horton's discussion of the essential distinction between the *educational* approach used at Highlander and the *organizing* approach implemented by Saul Alinsky in Myles Horton with Judith Kohl and Herbert Kohl, *The Long Haul: An Autobiography* (New York: Teacher's College Press, 1998), pp. 176–183.

31. Myles Horton with Judith Kohl and Herbert Kohl, *The Long Haul: An Autobiography* (New York: Teacher's College Press, 1998), and Myles Horton, "A Circle of Learners," in *The Myles Horton Reader: Education for Social Change*, ed. Dale Jacobs (Knoxville: University of Tennessee Press, 2003/1985).

32. Myles Horton with Judith Kohl and Herbert Kohl, *The Long Haul: An Autobiography* (New York: Teacher's College Press, 1998), p. 150.

33. The term "learning circle" was introduced to me by John Wallace from the University of Minnesota. He has tried to use the lessons for democratic education from Highlander in several community settings, including the creation of the Invisible College (now Educators for Community Engagement), the Jane Addams School for Democracy, and the Hope Work Folk School.

34. Quoted in Carl Tjerandsen, *Education for Citizenship: A Foundation's Experience* (Santa Cruz, California: Emil Schwarzhaupt Foundation, 1980), p. 166.

35. Myles Horton with Judith Kohl and Herbert Kohl, *The Long Haul: An Autobiography* (New York: Teacher's College Press, 1998), p. 160.

36. Paolo Freire, *Pedagogy of the Oppressed* (New York: Continuum, 2000/1970).

37. "Rough Notes" (Myles Horton Papers: Box 11, Folder 2, n.d.).

38. Myles Horton with Judith Kohl and Herbert Kohl, *The Long Haul: An Autobiography* (New York: Teacher's College Press, 1998), pp. 131–132.

39. Myles Horton, Notes (Horton Papers: Box 11, File 1, n.d.).

40. Myles Horton and Paulo Freire, *We Make the Road by Walking: Conversations on Education and Social Change* (Philadelphia: Temple University Press, 1990), pp. 99–100.

41. "Notes on What Is a Workshop and How to Plan It" (Horton Papers: Box 11, Folder 1, n.d.).

42. Ibid.

43. This process is described in Myles Horton with Judith Kohl and Herbert Kohl, *The Long Haul: An Autobiography* (New York: Teacher's College Press, 1998).

44. Myles Horton, "An Interview with Myles Horton: It's a Miracle—I Still Don't Believe It," *Phi Delta Kappan* (May 1966): 490–497.

45. Myles Horton, Notes (Horton Papers: Box 11, File 1, n.d.).

46. "Notes on Highlander Methods" (Highlander Papers: Box 11, Folder 1, n.d.).

47. "Notes on Highlander Methods" (Highlander Papers: Box 11, Folder 1, n.d.).

48. For a discussion of Zilphia Horton and the development and influence of folk music at Highlander, see Vicki K. Carter, "The Singing Heart of Highlander Folk School," in *New Horizons in Adult Education 8*, no. 2 (Spring 1994). See also Guy Carawan and Candie Carawan, "I'm Gonna Let It Shine: Singing at Highlander," *Social Policy 21*, no. 3 (Winter, 1991): 44–47.

49. For description of the citizenship schools, see the following: Frank Adams, *Unearthing Seeds of Fire: The Idea of Highlander* (Winston-Salem, North Carolina: John F. Blair, 1975); Cynthia Stokes Brown, ed., *Ready from Within: Septima Clark and the Civil Rights Movement* (Trenton, New Jersey: Africa World Press, 1990); John Glen, *Highlander: No Ordinary School* (Knoxville: The University of Tennessee Press, 1996); Aimee Horton, *The Highlander Folk School: A History of its Major Programs, 1932–1961* (Brooklyn: Carlson Publishing, 1989); Myles Horton with Judith Kohl and Herbert Kohl, *The Long Haul: An Autobiography* (New York: Teacher's College Press, 1998); and especially Carl Tjerandsen, *Education for Cit-*

izenship: A Foundation's Experience (Santa Cruz, California: Emil Schwarzhaupt Foundation, 1980).

50. Quoted in Cynthia Stokes Brown, ed., *Ready from Within: Septima Clark and the Civil Rights Movement* (Trenton, New Jersey: Africa World Press, 1990), p. 46.

51. Quoted in Carl Tjerandsen, *Education for Citizenship: A Foundation's Experience* (Santa Cruz, California: Emil Schwarzhaupt Foundation, 1980), pp. 151–152.

52. Carl Tjerandsen, *Education for Citizenship: A Foundation's Experience* (Santa Cruz, California: Emil Schwarzhaupt Foundation, 1980).

53. Quoted in Cynthia Stokes Brown, ed., *Ready from Within: Septima Clark and the Civil Rights Movement* (Trenton, New Jersey: Africa World Press, 1990), p. 45.

54. Cynthia Stokes Brown, ed., *Ready from Within: Septima Clark and the Civil Rights Movement* (Trenton, New Jersey: Africa World Press, 1990), p. 45.

55. Quoted in Cynthia Stokes Brown, ed., *Ready from Within: Septima Clark and the Civil Rights Movement* (Trenton, New Jersey: Africa World Press, 1990), p. 49.

56. Myles Horton with Judith Kohl and Herbert Kohl, *The Long Haul: An Autobiography* (New York: Teacher's College Press, 1998), p. 101.

57. Myles Horton with Judith Kohl and Herbert Kohl, *The Long Haul: An Autobiography* (New York: Teacher's College Press, 1998), p. 102.

58. Quoted in Cynthia Stokes Brown, ed., *Ready from Within: Septima Clark and the Civil Rights Movement* (Trenton, New Jersey: Africa World Press, 1990), p. 49.

59. Myles Horton, "Staff Memo" (Highlander Papers: Box 96, September 8, 1969).

60. Bernice Robinson quoted in Myles Horton with Judith Kohl and Herbert Kohl, *The Long Haul: An Autobiography* (New York: Teacher's College Press, 1998), p. 103.

61. See Aimee Horton, "A Workshop for Volunteer Teachers in the Citizenship Education Program of the Southern Christian Leadership Conference," in *An Analysis on Selected Programs for the Training of Civil Rights and Community Leaders in the South* (Horton Papers: Box 10, Folder 9, 1965), and Cynthia Stokes Brown, ed., *Ready from Within: Septima Clark and the Civil Rights Movement* (Trenton, New Jersey: Africa World Press, 1990).

62. Quoted in Aimee Horton, "A Workshop for Volunteer Teachers in the Citizenship Education Program of the Southern Christian Leadership Conference," in *An Analysis on Selected Programs for the Training of Civil Rights and Community Leaders in the South* (Horton Papers: Box 10, Folder 9, 1965), p. 97.

63. "Progress Report on the Citizenship School Program" (Highlander Papers: Box 38, January 27, 1961).

64. Carl Tjerandsen, *Education for Citizenship: A Foundation's Experience* (Santa Cruz, California: Emil Schwarzhaupt Foundation, 1980).

65. Septima Clark, "Letter to Myles Horton" (Highlander Papers: Box 38, Folder 2, 1960).

66. Ibid.

67. Ibid.

68. "Training Leaders for Citizenship Schools" (Highlander Papers: Box 38, n.d.).

69. Myles Horton with Judith Kohl and Herbert Kohl, *The Long Haul: An Autobiography* (New York: Teacher's College Press, 1998), pp. 138–139.

70. See Charles M. Payne, *I've Got the Light of Freedom: The Organizing Tradition and the Mississippi Freedom Struggle* (Los Angeles: University of California Press, 1995).

71. Septima Clark, "Southern Christian Leadership Conference Education Program (Horton Papers: Box 10, Folder 9, May 14, 1965).

72. Quoted in Carl Tjerandsen, *Education for Citizenship: A Foundation's Experience* (Santa Cruz, California: Emil Schwarzhaupt Foundation, 1980), pp. 180–181.

73. Harry C. Boyte and Nan Kari, *Building America: The Democratic Promise of Public Work* (Philadelphia: Temple University Press, 1996).

74. Dorothy Cotton quoted in Harry C. Boyte and Nan Kari, *Building America: The Democratic Promise of Public Work* (Philadelphia: Temple University Press, 1996), pp. 142-143.

75. Carl Tjerandsen, *Education for Citizenship: A Foundation's Experience* (Santa Cruz, California: Emil Schwarzhaupt Foundation, 1980), p. 201.

76. The similarities between the settlement house movement and civil rights movement are described by Harry C. Boyte and Nan Kari, *Building America: The Democratic Promise of Public Work* (Philadelphia: Temple University Press, 1996).

Chapter Five

Epigraph from Nan Skelton, telephone conversation with author, May 25, 2006.

1. Minnesota Public Radio, July 30, 2004.

2. Nan Kari, personal interview with author, July 27, 2004.

3. Nan Skelton et al., *A Community Alive with Learning: The Story of the West Side Neighborhood Learning Community 2001–2005* (Minneapolis: Center for Democracy and Citizenship, 2006). This chapter draws on this helpful report that outlines the lessons of the Neighborhood Learning Community.

4. Nan Skelton et al., *A Community Alive with Learning: The Story of the West Side Neighborhood Learning Community 2001–2005* (Minneapolis: Center for Democracy and Citizenship, 2006).

5. The term "culture of learning" was adapted by the Neighborhood Learning Community from the educational efforts of Jerome Stein, who coined the term to describe his experiences with the Prospect Park neighborhood of Minneapolis and the larger Learning Dreams initiative. See Jerome Stein, "A Community Model of Dropout Prevention—Revisited," *Community Education Journal*, no. 21 (1994): 18–20.

6. Nan Skelton et al., *A Community Alive with Learning: The Story of the West Side Neighborhood Learning Community 2001–2005* (Minneapolis: Center for Democracy and Citizenship, 2006), p. 7.

7. Nan Kari, personal interview with author, July 27, 2004.

8. Nan Skelton, personal interview with author, August 6, 2004.

9. The earlier history of West Side draws on "Those Were the Days," a chapter from Harry Boyte, *Community Is Possible: Repairing America's Roots* (New York: Harper & Row, 1984).

10. Quoted in Harry Boyte, *Community Is Possible: Repairing America's Roots* (New York: Harper & Row, 1984), p. 66.

11. Aleida Benitez, personal interview with author, May 29, 2006.

12. Neighborhood Learning Community Implementation Grant to Wallace Foundation (Center for Democracy and Citizenship: University of Minnesota, 2001).

13. John Wallace, personal interview with author, May 27, 1998.

14. For an excellent description of the public work tradition, see Harry C. Boyte and Nan Kari, *Building America: The Democratic Promise of Public Work* (Philadelphia: Temple University Press, 1996).

15. Canon Barnett and Henrietta Barnett, *Towards Social Reform* (New York: Macmillan, 1909), p. 286.

16. Nan Skelton, personal interview with author, August 6, 2004.

17. John Wallace, personal interview with author, May 27, 1998.

18. Nan Skelton, personal interview with author, August 6, 2004.

19. Nan Skelton with Nicholas V. Longo and Jennifer O'Donoghue, "Jane Addams School for Democracy," in *Creating the Commonwealth*, ed. Harry Boyte (Dayton: Kettering Foundation, 2000).

20. See, for example, Harry C. Boyte's chapter "The Jane Addams School for Democracy" in *Everyday Politics: Reconnecting Citizens and Public Life* (Philadelphia: University of Pennsylvania, 2004); John Wallace, "The Problem of Time: Enabling Students to Make Long-Term Commitments to Community-Based Learning," *Michigan Journal of Community Service Learning* 7 (2000): 133–142; Nicholas V. Longo, *Evaluation of Jane Addams School* (Minneapolis: Center for Urban and Regional Affairs and Center for Democracy and Citizenship, 1998); Nan Skelton with Nicholas V. Longo and Jennifer O'Donoghue, "Jane Addams School for Democracy," in *Creating the Commonwealth*, ed. Harry Boyte (Dayton: Kettering Foundation, 2000); and eds. Nan Skelton and Nan Kari, *Voices of Hope: The Story of the Jane Addams School for Democracy* (Dayton: Kettering Foundation, 2007).

21. Terri Wilson, personal interview with author, August, 1998, and Terri Wilson, "A Call to Vocation," in eds. Nan Skelton and Nan Kari, *Voices of Hope: the Story of the Jane Addams School for Democracy* (Dayton: Kettering Foundation, 2007).

22. Koua Yang Her, personal interview with author, August 3, 1998.

23. Nan Skelton, personal interview with author, August 6, 2004.

24. Kari Denissen, personal interview with author, July 27, 2004.

25. Elona Street Stewart, personal interview with author, August 5, 2004.

26. Ibid.

27. Jerome Stein, "Youth Development in Context: Education in the Community," in *The University and the Community: Renewing the Relationship*, eds. Jerome Stein and Nicholas V. Longo (Minneapolis: Center for 4–H Youth Development, University of Minnesota, 2001), p. 10. See also John Dewey, *The School and Society* (Chicago: University of Chicago Press, 1990/1899).

28. Anne T. Henderson and Karen L. Mapp, *A New Wave of Evidence: The Impact of School, Family, and Community Connections on Student Achievement* (Austin: Southwest Educational Development Laboratory, 2002).

29. Lawrence Steinberg, *Beyond the Classroom: Why School Reform Has Failed and What Parents Need to Do* (New York: Simon & Schuster, 1996), p. 194.

30. Susan L. Dauber and Joyce Epstein, "Parent Attitudes and Practices of Involvement in Inner-City Elementary and Middle Schools," in *Families and Schools in a Pluralistic Society*, ed. Nancy Charkin (Albany: State University of New York Press, 1993), pp. 53–71; and Anne T. Henderson and Nancy Berla, *A New Generation of Evidence: The Family Is Critical to Student Achievement* (Columbia: National Committee for Citizens in Education, 1994).

31. See Jerome Stein, J. "A Community Model of Dropout Prevention—Revisited," *Community Education Journal*, no. 21 (1994): 18–20.

32. Dennis Shirley, *Community Organizing for Urban School Reform* (Austin: University of Texas Press, 1997), p. 72.

33. Ibid., p. 73.

34. Ibid., p. 76.

35. Personal interview with author, July 30, 2004.

36. For good histories of school reform, see Lawrence Cremin, *The Transformation of the School: Progressive Education in American Education 1876–1957* (New York: Vintage Books, 1961) and John I. Goodlad, *In Praise of Education* (New York: Teachers College Press, 1997).

37. Harry C. Boyte, *Everyday Politics: Reconnecting Citizens and Public Life* (Philadelphia: University of Pennsylvania, 2004).

38. Mary Margaret Sullivan, personal interview with author, August 2, 2004.

39. Bob Cudahy, personal interview with author, August 4, 2004.

40. Quoted in Nan Skelton et al., *A Community Alive with Learning: The Story of the West Side Neighborhood Learning Community 2001–2005* (Minneapolis: Center for Democracy and Citizenship, 2006), p. 20.

41. Ibid., p. 23.

42. *The Civic Mission of Schools* (New York: Carnegie Corporation and Center for Information and Research on Civic Learning and Engagement, 2003); Scott Keeter et al., *The Civic and Political Health of the Nation: A Generational Portrait* (College Park, Maryland: Center for Information and Research on Civic Learning and Engagement, 2002); and William Galston, "Political Knowledge, Political Engagement, and Civic Education," *Annual Review of Political Science 4* (2001) 217–234.

43. Aleida Benitez, personal interview with author, October 25, 2004.

44. Chao Moua quote from panel discussion at West Side Conference, May 1, 2006, and Nan Skelton et al., *A Community Alive with Learning: The Story of the West Side Neighborhood Learning Community 2001–2005* (Minneapolis: Center for Democracy and Citizenship, 2006).

45. Nan Skelton et al., *A Community Alive with Learning: The Story of the West Side Neighborhood Learning Community 2001–2005* (Minneapolis: Center for Democracy and Citizenship, 2006).

46. Nan Kari, personal interview with author, July 27, 2004.

47. Kari Denissen, personal interview with author, July 27, 2004.

48. Quoted in Nan Skelton et al., *A Community Alive with Learning: The Story of the West Side Neighborhood Learning Community 2001–2005* (Minneapolis: Center for Democracy and Citizenship, 2006).

49. The quotes from this section are all taken from four focus groups conducted by the author with youths involved in the Youth Apprenticeship Project and Youth Farm and Market Project on July 29, 2004, and August 5, 2004.

50. Elona Street Stewart, personal interview with author, August 5, 2004.

51. Ibid.

52. Harry C. Boyte, *Everyday Politics: Reconnecting Citizens and Public Life* (Philadelphia: University of Pennsylvania, 2004), p. xi.

53. Ibid., p. 12.

54. Personal interview with author, July 27, 2004.

55. Nan Kari, personal interview with author, July 27, 2004.

56. Nan Skelton et al., *A Community Alive with Learning: The Story of the West Side Neighborhood Learning Community 2001–2005* (Minneapolis: Center for Democracy and Citizenship, 2006).

57. Malcolm Gladwell, *The Tipping Point: How Little Things Can Make a Big Difference* (Boston: Back Bay Books, 2000).

58. Kari Denissen, personal interview with author, July 27, 2004.

59. Personal interview with author, August 2, 2004.

60. Harry C. Boyte, *Everyday Politics: Reconnecting Citizens and Public Life* (Philadelphia: University of Pennsylvania, 2004), p. 85.

61. Harry C. Boyte, *Everyday Politics: Reconnecting Citizens and Public Life* (Philadelphia: University of Pennsylvania, 2004); Tom Webb, "Project Is Democracy in Action" *Pioneer Press*, February 1, 2004, C1.

62. Tom Webb, "Project Is Democracy in Action," *Pioneer Press*, February 1, 2004, p. 4C.

63. Personal interview with author, July 30, 2004.

64. Deborah Meier, *In Schools We Trust: Creating Communities of Learning in an Era of Testing and Standization* (Boston: Beacon Press, 2002).

65. Personal interview with author, July 26, 2004; personal interview with author, July 30, 2004.

66. Nan Kari, personal interview with author, January 5, 2005.

Chapter Six

Epigraph from Lisbeth Schorr, *Common Purpose: Strengthening Families and Neighborhoods to Rebuild America* (New York: Anchor Books, 1997), p. 12.

1. Harry C. Boyte and Nan Kari describe "public work" in *Building America: The Democratic Promise of Public Work* (Philadelphia: Temple University Press, 1996); Lisbeth Schorr details "new practitioners" in *Common Purpose: Strengthening Families and Neighborhoods to Rebuild America* (New York: Anchor Books, 1997); Jerome Stein uses "community builders" in "Community Youth Development: New Challenges for a New Century," *The Center: University of Minnesota Extension Service* (Fall 2000): 18–23; and Malcolm Gladwell examines "community connectors" in *The Tipping Point: How Little Things Can Make a Big Difference* (Boston: Back Bay Books, 2000).

2. Donald Schön, *The Reflective Practitioner: How Professionals Think in Action* (New York: Basic Books, 1983) and Donald Schön, *Educating the Reflective Practitioner: Toward a New Design for Teaching and Learning in the Professions* (San Francisco: Jossey-Bass, 1987). See also Tony Jeffs and Mark Smith, *Informal Education: Conversation, Democracy, and Learning* (London: Education Now Publishing, 1999).

3. Donald Schön, *The Reflective Practitioner: How Professionals Think in Action* (New York: Basic Books, 1983), p. 19.

4. Donald Schön, *Educating the Reflective Practitioner: Toward a New Design for Teaching and Learning in the Professions* (San Francisco: Jossey-Bass, 1987), p. 5.

5. Jerome Stein, "Community Youth Development: New Challenges for a New Century, *The Center: University of Minnesota Extension Service* (Fall 2000): 18–23, esp. 22.

6. Malcolm Gladwell, *The Tipping Point: How Little Things Can Make a Big Difference* (Boston: Back Bay Books, 2000), p. 54. See also Malcolm Gladwell, "Six Degrees of Lois Weisberg," *The New Yorker,* January 11, 1999.

7. Malcolm Gladwell, *The Tipping Point: How Little Things Can Make a Big Difference* (Boston: Back Bay Books, 2000), pp. 36–37.

8. The definition of informal education comes from Tony Jeffs and Mark Smith, *Informal Education: Conversation, Democracy, and Learning* (London: Education Now Publishing, 1999), p. 19.

9. Leonard Covello, "The School as the Center of Community Life in an Immigrant Area," in *The Community School*, ed. Samuel Everett (New York: D. Appleton-Century Company, 1938), p. 127.

10. Kari Denissen, personal interview with author, July 27, 2004.

11. Jerome Stein, "Youth Development in Context: Education in the Community," in *The University and the Community: Renewing the Relationship*, eds. Jerome Stein and Nicholas V. Longo (Minneapolis: Center for 4–H Youth Development, University of Minnesota, 2001), p. 11.

12. Personal interview with author, July 28, 2004.

13. For a discussion of local knowledge, see James Scott, *Seeing Like a State: How Certain Schemes to Improve the Human Condition Have Failed* (New Haven: Yale University Press, 1998).

14. See John Kretzmann and John McKnight, *Building Communities from the Inside Out: A Path Toward Finding and Mobilizing a Community's Assets* (Chicago: ACTA Publications, 1993) and also John McKnight, *The Careless Society: Community and Its Counterfeits* (New York: Basic Books, 1995).

15. For an overview of the Center for Democracy and Citizenship's work, see www.publicwork.org.

16. Mark Smith, *Local Education: Community, Conversation, Praxis* (Philadelphia: Open University Press, 1994), p. 7.

17. "Being local" is both a tool and a mindset as described by Jerome Stein and others. See *Advancing Youth Development: A Community Approach* [TC Best Facilitator's Guide] (Minneapolis: Center for 4–H Youth Development, 2000) and Mark Smith, *Local Education: Community, Conversation, Praxis* (Philadelphia: Open University Press, 1994).

18. Mark Smith, *Local Education: Community, Conversation, Praxis* (Philadelphia: Open University Press, 1994), p. 15.

19. *Advancing Youth Development: A Community Approach* [TC Best Facilitator's Guide] (Minneapolis: Center for 4–H Youth Development, 2000), p. 58.

20. Mark Smith, *Local Education: Community, Conversation, Praxis* (Philadelphia: Open University Press, 1994), pp. 92–93.

21. Robert Scott, "A Student Again: Leading from Within," *The Chronicle of Higher Education*, January 18, 2002.

22. See Charles M. Payne, *I've Got the Light of Freedom: The Organizing Tradition and the Mississippi Freedom Struggle* (Los Angeles: University of California Press, 1995), p. 75.

Chapter Seven

Epigraph from Theodore Sizer, *The Red Pencil: Convictions from Experience in Education* (New Haven: Yale University Press, 2004), p. 24.

1. Yvonna Lincoln and Norman Denzin, "The Fifth Moment," in *Handbook of Qualitative Research*, eds. Norman Denzin and Yvonna Lincoln (London: Sage Publications, 1994), p. 584.

2. For a well-developed argument for a different kind of politics, see Harry C. Boyte, "A Different Kind of Politics: John Dewey and the Meaning of Citizenship in the 21st Century," speech presented at the University of Michigan, November 1, 2002. For lessons on scaling innovation up, see Lisbeth Schorr, *Common Purpose: Strengthening Families and Neighborhoods to Rebuild America* (New York: Anchor Books, 1997).

3. Ira Harkavy and Marty Blank, "Community Schools: A Vision of Learning that Goes Beyond Testing," *Education Week*, April 17, 2002, p. 22.

4. Robert Halpern *Rebuilding the Inner City: A History of Neighborhood Initiatives to Address Poverty in the United States* (New York: Columbia University Press, 1995), p. 5.

5. *New York Times*, "Jane Addams," May 22, 1935.

6. Comprehensive, relational, and public education, as described in chapter one, comes from Lawrence Cremin, *Public Education* (New York: Basic Books, 1976).

7. Jane Addams, "The Objective Value of a Social Settlement," in *The Social Thought of Jane Addams*, ed. Christopher Lasch (New York: Bobbs-Merrill, 1965/1892).

8. Jane Addams, *Democracy and Social Ethics* (Chicago: University of Illinois Press, 2002/1902).

9. Jane Addams, *The Long Road of Woman's Memory* (Chicago: University of Illinois Press, 2002/1916).

10. Jane Addams, *Democracy and Social Ethics* (Chicago: University of Illinois Press, 2002/1902).

11. Nan Kari, quoted in Harry Boyle, *Everyday Politics* (Philadelphia: University of Pennsylvania, 2004), p. 112.

12. Septima Clark, "Letter to Myles Horton" (Highlander Papers: Box 38, Folder 2, 1960).

13. This, of course, took place prior to the professionalization of social work, a development Addams fought. See Christopher Lasch, *Revolt of the Elites* (New York: Norton, 1995) and Andrew Polsky *The Rise of the Therapeutic State* (Princeton: Princeton University Press, 1991).

14. For the problems of technocratic interventions, see James C. Scott, *Seeing Like a State: How Certain Schemes to Improve the Human Condition Have Failed* (New Haven: Yale University Press, 1998) and Anne Fadiman, *The Spirit Catches You and You Fall Down* (New York: Farrar, Straus, and Giroux, 1997).

15. John Wallace, personal interview with author, May 27, 1998.

16. Nan Skelton, quoted in Harry C. Boyte, *Everyday Politics: Reconnecting Citizens and Public Life* (Philadelphia: University of Pennsylvania, 2004), p. 105.

17. Personal interview with author, August 5, 2004.

18. Quoted in Harry C. Boyte, *Everyday Politics: Reconnecting Citizens and Public Life* (Philadelphia: University of Pennsylvania, 2004), p. 99.

19. Quoted in Myles Horton with Judith Kohl and Herbert Kohl, *The Long Haul: An Autobiography* (New York: Teacher's College Press, 1998), p. 103.

20. Jane Addams, "The Subjective Necessity for Social Settlements," in *The Jane Addams Reader*, ed. Jean Bethke Elshtain (New York: Basic Books, 2002/1893), p. 14.

21. Myles Horton with Judith Kohl and Herbert Kohl, *The Long Haul: An Autobiography* (New York: Teacher's College Press, 1998), p. 157.

22. Jane Addams, "The Subjective Necessity for Social Settlements," in *The Jane Addams Reader*, ed. Jean Bethke Elshtain (New York: Basic Books, 2002/1893), p. 26.

23. Ira Harkavy, "Governance and the Connection Between Community, Higher Education, and Schools," in *Gathering Momentum: Building the Learning Connection Between Schools and Colleges* (proceedings of the Learning Connections Conference, Kansas City, Missouri, April 2002): 20–29.

24. To get a sense of the complexity of school reform, see Seymour Sarason, *The Predictable Failure of Educational Reform: Can We Change Course Before It's Too Late?* (San Francisco: Jossey-Bass, 1990).

25. *Renewing the Covenant: Learning, Discovery and Engagement in a New Age and a Different World* (Kellogg Commission on the Future of State and Land-Grant Universities, 2000), p. 24.

26. The service scholarship programs at Bentley College, DePaul University, and IUPUI are described in chapters in Edward Zlotkowski, Nicholas V. Longo, and James Williams, eds., *Students as Colleagues: Expanding the Circle of Service-Learning Leadership* (Providence: Campus Compact, 2006).

Index